Heather,

Never settle for less
than your able!! You
deserve God's best!
Great Spring,
Bill Cantrell

Finding Your Direction

Seven Stages to Fulfilling
Your Life's Work
With Integrity

Bill Cantrell, CSP

with Karen S. Anderson, MS

Published by
Legacy Communications Group, Inc.
251 Second Avenue South
Franklin, Tennessee 37064

Finding Your Direction —
Proven Secrets to Fulfilling Your Life's Work With Integrity

ISBN 1-884067-08-5

All Scripture quotes are taken from the King James Bible unless otherwise noted.

Books are available in quantity for promotional or premium use. For information on discount and terms write to Director of Special Sales, Legacy Communications Group, Inc., 251 Second Avenue South, Franklin, Tennessee 37064.

Manufactured in the United States of America.

CONTENTS

DEDICATION

Dedicated to my parents,

Bill and Sue Cantrell,

for giving me roots and wings,

Long before it was a catchy phrase.

And to William J. McGrane Jr.

for helping me find *my*

direction in life.

ACKNOWLEDGMENTS

This book is the product of 20 years in the training and consulting business and countless people who have shaped my thinking and helped me become who I am. I'd like to thank my mother and father for their example, love, guidance and enormous support. Thanks to Coach Bud Garrett, who taught me that function follows form and nothing great comes without personal sacrifice and discipline, also, a big thanks to Ms. Mary Louise Aste, my Latin teacher, who convinced me I could learn.

And many thanks to Don Hutson, Dr. Wayland Tonning and Dr. Paul Green, who were local hero's growing up. I appreciate David Cooper, Sandy Karn, Zig Ziglar, and Cavett Robert for helping me find my way to and through the Rally Days with the Positive Thinking Rallies.

Special appreciations goes to William J. McGrane and the McGrane Institute for demonstrating how to live what I believe and impact the lives of others in a deeper way. To Bill McGrane III for his support and friendship. And to Jason Hannath and G. David Small, for helping this book idea become a reality.

A very special thanks to Karen Anderson for her willingness to live this manuscript with me and her spiritual commitment to this project that went far beyond any hope for financial gain, and to Steve Anderson for his "Tech support." I appreciate the shaping influence of Ruth Ann Arnold and her special touch as an accomplished author in helping me tell my story!

Then I want to appreciate Cecilia and Doug Belew at Paragon Communications Group, Inc. for their expertise in designing the cover and layout plus enormous editing contributions. I want to thank John and Brenda Ward for their friendship and their publishing, editing and writing expertise so freely given. Thanks for all the encouragement.

Thanks to my publisher, David Dunham at Legacy Communications for helping initiate the project and for helping it come to fruition. I'd also like to acknowledge Todd Rutherford for his feedback, encouragement and marketing expertise.

I'd like to thank my staff, Marie Pressley, Tom Carney, Donna Osborn and Vicki Goad for their patience and understanding and also for their support of me as much of my focus and time became devoted to this project.

A very heart-felt lump in my throat and sense of gratitude and thanksgiving goes to my talented wife, Kay, who has always "covered" for me so I can do what I love so much. Honey, thanks for being the perfect partner in life and business. To my lovely daughters, Katie and Kristen, thanks for being so patient and generous with dad and for making it so easy for me to live a more balanced and abundant life full of joy and wonder. You're both so much fun I don't want to miss a minute with you.

FINDING YOUR DIRECTION

What is my direction here on earth?
Something that's determined for me from birth?
I think not, sometimes as I make my way,
So many things surprise me on a given day.

If I have a direction at all, could it be determined
By simply accepting my quiet inner call?
Do we allow our environment to decide the path we take?
Or do we accept responsibility for every decision that we make?

What has happened to us may be neither here nor there.
What really makes our direction clear is choosing to take the dare.
We know many times what we really want and need to do
Then allow outside forces to keep us from seeing it through.

I once reflected on the time in my life
when pain played the greatest part.
Now I ask myself how this event was destined from the start.
Could it be the lesson I need the most is planted with that seed?
My acorn planted, I nurture it forth and choose the life I lead.

This acorn has the making of a mighty oak inside
If we only water and protect it so its branches can grow wide.
My direction is not determined by those things that happened to me,
Yet what I do from that point on will secure my destiny.

Bill Cantrell

CHAPTER I

Seeds

A full-grown oak tree, with its broad branches and towering height, has its full genetic coding within the little acorn seed. The tiny seed contains all the potential for a full, mature tree. What if the same were true of us?

We have the potential within to fully develop, grow and learn. We can all become mighty, majestic, and well-developed like the oak tree.

Unfortunately, not all acorns become full grown oak trees! What prevents them from reaching maturity and developing into what they have the potential to become? I believe there are many things that happen along the way that can prevent the acorn from fulfilling its created purpose. The acorn could be stolen by a squirrel before it gets a chance to germinate, be crushed underfoot by a person walking by, or it could be drowned out by a raging storm. And sometimes, even when the tree does grow, it doesn't grow to its full capacity.

The path of the tiny seed doesn't seem so different from the path you and I take to mature to our potential. There are issues with which we have to contend in our lives that influence things that we do. Many times, events that influence us the most occurred early in our lives. Although, many of our "seedling" experiences affect us for the rest of our life, they also prepare us for what is ahead. However, many of us have never stopped to discover how our early experiences impact our lives today.

When I began my career in sales, I quickly realized I needed to look at the reasons I feel and behave the way I do, in order to overcome the obstacles that were preventing me from getting where I wanted to go. As I analyzed some of the events in my life, I made some discoveries that were very useful. Research indicates that even things that happened *before* we are born can have an influence on us. In the book *The Secret Life of the Unborn Child*, the author provides evidence of the ability that unborn babies have to pick up on signals and feelings.

One mother says her baby was born patient, serene, and a contemplative little philosopher. A father says his daughter was a squirming and restless acrobat from the first moment.

It's clear, newborn babies differ in a variety of observable ways. For example, because there have been no experiences outside the womb known to have exerted their influence, these differences can be traced to the combined effects of three factors: (1) the basic genetic endowment bestowed by the parents, (2) the normal course of an individual's intrauterine development, and (3) the circumstances of birth itself. Yet what are the possible influences on development in the womb? We know the "pre-born child" and its maternal environment begin interacting at conception in a process that continues throughout adult life:

> Slowly, the old nature-nurture controversy—the question as to whether heredity or environment is more important—is being recognized as a non-issue. What is emerging instead is a complementary theory of life, where genes and environment work together. The genes determine the range of potential possibilities: and the environment selects among them. Thus, for example, genes may dictate that someone grows to a height between five-feet-eight-inches and six-feet-one-inch; but diet, hygiene, stress and general health will determine the precise point at which growth stops.
>
> Dr. Zsolt Harsanyi, *Cornell Medical Center,* and
> Richard Hutton, *medical writer*

When my wife, Kay, and I were expecting our first child, we were like many first time parents—totally entranced by this new little person. I remember, before going to sleep at night, I'd lie in bed with Kay and watch the baby move and kick and do somersaults. Early in the pregnancy, I began to speak to the baby saying, "This is your father speaking," and then I would sing a little song. This became a regular routine as she grew and got ready to make her entrance into the world.

When she finally arrived, the first thing I said to her was, "Katie, this is your father speaking, welcome to our world!" To my amazement, and utter delight, she turned her little head toward me and opened one little eye the moment she heard my voice. Although some may think this was a coincidence, I *knew* she recognized my voice from the many times I had spoken to her.

OUR FAMILY TREE

Recently, I was in the waiting room of my children's pediatrician filling out paperwork. I noticed how many questions were asked about our family's medical history and background. For example: "Has anyone in your family ever had heart disease, high blood pressure or cancer?" Obviously, our family history plays a significant part in who we are. Our genetic programming is what we arrive with at birth.

Our own predispositions may be cerebral, athletic, active, passive, vocal, quiet, needy, satisfied, high maintenance, low maintenance, determined, melancholy, joyful, outgoing, reserved, or a variety of other things. These predispositions influence, to some degree, the issues with which we will contend as we move into our life's work and chosen profession.

DISCOVERING OUR SEEDS

The events and circumstances that have influenced our life can be referred to as seeds. What are the seeds that determine the direction we follow for our life in general, and how do they affect the choices we make in our work or businesses?

These seeds can be either affirming or non affirming influences. They can be a predisposition to an internal behavioral challenge such as lack of confidence or motivation, or to an external circumstance such as lack of education, poverty or a physical challenge. Fortunately, they can also be invaluable beneficial qualities and characteristics that empower us to face challenges in such a manner that the end result is victory. Persistence, faith, confidence, curiosity, helpfulness and a willingness to learn can be seeds that propel us toward our chosen direction.

We need to evaluate our seeds and how they influence our direction. This evaluation will allow us to balance, in our heart and mind, the seeds planted in the past. A tendency or predisposition in one direction may be based on interpreting seeds as preparation for the future. No matter what types of seeds have been planted, it is critical that we evaluate and accept responsibility for nurturing those that can benefit us in our development.

ASSESSING YOUR SEEDS

Recently, I discovered one of the seeds in my life. Someone asked me about the circumstances when I was born. I realized I didn't really know anything about my birth and so I asked my mother some questions. I learned that she had been quite ill when she was pregnant with me. In fact, she was so sick the doctors prescribed a number of prescription medications for her to take. In the early '50s, the medical community wasn't aware of the impact of drugs on unborn children. It wasn't until the 1960s, when the prescription drug Thalidomide™ was given to pregnant women, and their babies were born with severe birth defects, that the full effects of medication on the developing fetus were realized. Today, health experts agree that tobacco products have an adverse effect on unborn children. Studies show that even one puff of a cigarette can have a definable physiological effect—a two minute miniature convulsion—on an unborn baby.

During my conversation with my mother, she mentioned that, shortly after I was delivered, I had uncontrollable tremors. The doctors had told my parents that they thought I might have cerebral palsy. It turned out to be a withdrawal from the powerful drugs my mother had been prescribed. From what my mother recalls, these symptoms lasted for four or five months before they subsided. My mother wasn't able to hold and cuddle her newborn the way she wanted to. It's got to be tough to bond with a shaking, shivering baby, crying his little lungs out for hours at a time—imagine the long sleepless nights.

With difficult circumstances like this, most parents just love their babies through any trials that they face; others may snap, lose control or become depressed. Whatever the case may be, babies have impressionable little minds. So I ask you to consider, "What does a baby think? What does a baby feel toward his or her environment?" Is it acceptance or is it rejection?

WELCOME TO THE WORLD

Cavett Robert, the great speaker and humanitarian, said we spend the first nine months of our life on a waterbed with food and water piped in. Most of us have a safe, warm, comfortable place to stay, where we can lay back, relax and soak up the atmosphere. Then, suddenly, whether we are ready or not, we are pushed out of bed and forced into a tight cramped spot for a long slow trip into a freezing cold blinding light. As soon as we arrive, the doctor lifts us up by our heels upside down and, with a spanking, says, "Welcome to our world." Next, they do a terrible thing, they cut our cord. Cavett says many of us are so traumatized, after all this, that we spend the rest of our lives wandering around looking for another place to plug it in.

My pediatrician was Dr. William Crook, the now renowned author of the best selling book *The Yeast Connection.* One night, when my parents were totally exhausted and at their wits end, Dr. Crook came over around midnight to take care of me so my parents could get some much needed rest—those were the days when doctors made house calls!

Dr. Crook diagnosed me as having multiple food allergies including allergies to mother's milk and cow's milk. Although I was put on soy formula and goat's milk, the enamel on my teeth didn't develop so they quickly decayed. Then because my teeth had fallen out early from decay, my permanent teeth came in quite creatively, giving me a unique look all my own, requiring years of braces and extensive dental work. My poor parents had quite a lot to contend with!

I discovered, after learning this information from my mother, that my early environment was not exactly a friendly place. Despite the fact that my parents loved and wanted me, my world was hostile. And because of that, I think my challenge with rejection started very early on in my life.

DEALING WITH REJECTION

As I began my career in sales, it became increasingly obvious that dealing with rejection and handling the "no's" was not going to be easy. In highly competitive business environments, our feelings of rejection surface in similar ways as we try to figure out our value, worth, and where we fit into the scheme of things. We often look at status, position and external "trappings" that we believe define us in our work environment. We often succumb to the temptation of comparing ourselves with others, compromising a healthy sense of self respect—and obscuring the gifts, abilities and talents that are unique to us.

Many times we make decisions in business to protect ourselves from rejection or getting hurt, instead of basing them on the merits of the situation. To be successful in business, we need to make decisions that reflect our own best "choice of direction". Do not be governed by fear of rejection or failure.

Until we learn how to deal with the fear of rejection, or other issues that stand in our way, it is far too easy to choose a life of approval and acceptance, never really having the courage to meet our potential.

WAYS REJECTION AFFECTS US

When asked, "What is it in particular about rejection that bothers you so much?", many people respond by saying that it means "I am not okay or good enough." Many people think that something they have done is unacceptable, or that they have made a mistake and therefore the result they desired didn't occur. A common reaction to rejection is to point the finger at ourselves almost *immediately*. Rejection makes us feel unimportant or that we have let down the people who depend on us.

Rejection or not closing a sale can plant a seed that discourages self-confidence. It fans the fire of our low self-esteem. We may start thinking "What if I'm not up to this?" No is the one simple word that instantly reminds us of our fear. With so many non-affirming people and circumstances around us, it is critical that we learn to overcome any feeling of rejection. By doing so, we can turn those rejection feelings into learned lessons that will bring positive results.

HEALTHY WAYS TO OVERCOME REJECTION

Getting over rejection means not only getting beyond it, however discovering ways to provide some insulation or internal protection. When we are able to adequately protect ourselves, we can increase our activity level as well as the numbers of people with whom we do business. When we are out in the field, constantly being rejected and not knowing how to handle it or what to do, time becomes an enemy. We procrastinate, drift, or fail to stay focused. We feel, at a subconscious level, that if we don't make any new calls, we can successfully avoid being rejected once again.

However, this approach is death to our bottom line and our business!

We come up with some very clever ways to avoid rejection. One is to think that since "value" is subjective, we can use it as an excuse to shun talking to prospects—for fear they will either think what we are offering is priced too high or by "believing" that they don't really need what we are offering. If we fall into the trap of "sizing our potential customers up" *before* we help them determine if what we have to offer is of value for them, we are seeking to avoid rejection.

We may say to ourselves, "You know, I'll bet they are busy. Maybe they just got home from work or they're just sitting down to dinner. I better play it safe and call tomorrow." What torture! We need to give people a chance to say yes, no, or maybe for themselves—we need to let them decide.

Simply put, value over cost means that its relative importance for me is higher than the price to acquire it. Our customers need to determine the value for themselves. Our challenge as sales people becomes gradually educating and building the value of what our product or service offers to help them make a decision to buy.

HOW FEAR PATTERNS DEVELOP

One essential idea I learned twenty years ago when I began my sales career was how to deal *effectively* with rejection. Rejection typically happens in sales, however this idea also applies to personal relationships as well as other business and management situations. I affectionately refer to it as "falling in love with the no's!"

Let me explain.

When you offer your product or service and someone says "no", how do you feel? Is it no big deal and you move on, or does hearing "no" make you want to do anything except go to the next prospect and ask the same question again?

Ask yourself, "What is it about hearing the word 'no' that bothers me?"

Many of us would say that, when we hear "no", we feel the rejection is a *personal* reflection on us. More often than not, when rejection occurs time after time, we begin to shut down, becoming overly sensitive to anything that might create more rejection. We become extraordinarily busy, and that doesn't mean we are *productive*.

When we are busy, yet unproductive, we simply exchange safe, non-threatening activities for ones that could potentially be productive and involve rejection. This sets up an avoidance pattern creating an internal conflict between our need to protect ourselves and the knowledge that we are doing less than we are able. Shakespeare stated, "Our doubts and fears are traitors that make us lose the best we oft might gain by fearing to attempt." I believe when fear motivates us to settle for less than we are capable of becoming, we *dramatically* shortchange ourselves.

FALLING IN LOVE WITH THE "NO'S"

Rejection doesn't have to stop us from completing our plan or keep us from taking action. We can learn to deal with rejection in such a way that the "no's" don't have to bother us again. Your background, your beginnings or your circumstances do not have to stop you. I'm confident that if I can learn to deal with rejection so can you!

The first thing you want to do as a sales person is to get your prospect to give you the time of day! He or she may not know that your product is valuable, no matter how much you believe in its worth. The first challenge is to initiate a relationship, building trust and rapport. A sales person earns the opportunity to educate a prospect about the product or service. It doesn't happen automatically; it happens when we shift our focus to the clients and their needs and away from ourselves. We need to move beyond the fear of rejection in order to place our priorities in the correct place.

THE IDEA THAT MADE THE DIFFERENCE

As a frontline salesperson, my survival depended upon coming up with a way to maintain my personal integrity (being true to myself and not settling for less) and at the same time, being able to handle frequent rejection. When I placed monetary value on my activity level, I could maintain—and even increase—my productivity even in the midst of a rejection environment. Now regardless of the outcome, I could come away without feeling devastated because I didn't allow fear to compromise focus.

SUCCESSFULLY DETACHING OURSELVES

There's a process all of us go through to figure out the reason for a no response. We usually ask ourselves the following questions:

• *Could it be the company I represent?* No. The company is first class. They do things in a professional manner, they have their client's best interest at heart, and they have high standards.

• *Could it be the product or service?* No. The product or service is one of the best in the business. It's proven to be sought after and is highly successful.

• *Could it be me?* We come to the conclusion that there's something we are doing "wrong." We think that if we modify the presentation or change our timing, maybe it would work.

So in response, we stop working, start analyzing and try to figure out what's going on with us before we try again. We end up never calling to promote our new venture, product or service because we don't want to deal with more rejection.

What if it's not the company, the product or us?

• *Could it be them?* It only makes sense that if they knew what we know about our product and they felt the same way we do it would be easier for them to say "yes." What if they simply need more *information?*

Most likely, it doesn't have anything to do with whether or not they *like* you! Instead, they might not have enough information to place the proper value on your product or service. At first, the price may seem high while the apparent value is small. The client does not have enough information to make an educated decision. Therefore, the initial reaction is actually appropriate for that situation.

THE PRICE TO VALUE FACTOR

It is our responsibility to educate people and begin to build *value,* instructing how this particular product or service could make a difference in their life. We do this by layering information—a process that usually takes place one layer at a time. It's extremely difficult to educate people (let alone convince or persuade them that our product is beneficial for them) if we don't have more than one contact!

Here's where we can redefine ourselves. We are in the business of *educating people* about the value of our product, service or idea. So, even if they say "no", we can ask them:

"Would it be okay if I keep in contact with you from time to time to let you know other ways this might benefit you or to let you know about new products or upcoming opportunities?"

There are many people who would say "yes" if for no other reason than they feel uncomfortable telling *you* no! Some people might say okay to ease their own conscience about turning down an opportunity before learning all the facts!

If someone does say "yes" on the first call, then can we presume we are the one who *sold* them? Or did they already have enough information to make a decision and we just happened to be there at the proper time and place? There are many ways people find out about a product—from other customers, advertising or they may have had previous experience with the company or its products. If they are pre-sold, we are just taking the order!

When somebody says "no", that's when the educational selling process of transferring knowledge and value begins!

BUILDING VALUE

Even if we believe our product will make a difference in their lives, the customers need to conclude that for *themselves.*

We educate them by transferring our knowledge, feelings and beliefs to them by layering information one layer at a time. The best way to communicate your belief in your product or service is by your persistence. If fear of rejection stops us from persisting, we ultimately do a disservice to our customers. Even worse, we communicate to them that we don't really believe in what we do. Furthermore, we communicate that same message to ourselves.

Keeping in touch is the vehicle to convey your commitment to meeting their needs and serving them. If we know that value is built layer by layer through shared information, then regular contact is essential to open the lines of communication.

MAKING EVERY CONTACT MAKE YOU MONEY

The following idea changed my perception of the meaning of "no" and put it in proper perspective. This is where my "romance" with the "no's" began.

When we are working on commission, we know that if we don't follow through and maintain a healthy activity level, we lose money. If we don't make a contact, in essence, we are temporarily out of a job! Making a contact and receiving a no response doesn't mean that it wasn't worth our time. What if we were to get paid for that activity regardless of the response? If we put the emphasis on effort, instead of outcome, wouldn't it be easier to keep on making contacts?

Many of the great pioneers in sales training, have proposed an excellent idea for reinterpreting rejection. It involves something called "determining your call average". I have found that this brilliant idea has made a significant change in how I feel when I get a "no" from a prospect. So I took the original concept and developed a more comprehensive system of mental and emotional protection.

DETERMINE YOUR CALL AVERAGE

Are you aware of your per call average? If you have a proposal or you are sending out a sample chapter of a book to get published, do you know your ratio of rejection to acceptance? In simple terms, how many no's vs. how many yeses does it take to make a sale? How many contacts do you need to make before you get the outcome that you want?

Here's a way to place a monetary value on your activity level. Let's say you make ten calls or contacts and you get one $400 sale. To make this simple, with a 50 percent commission, you are making $200 or $20 *per contact*. This means that whether they say "yes" or "no", you still make $20 per call. If you make $20 per call, how much do you make on the "yes"? The answer is $20, because it only represents one call... "the last one."

One of the little known secrets of selling is that the "yes" always comes on the last call! *You can't get the "yes" without the "no",* If you could, you'd go straight to the "yes!"

The "no's" end up being a necessary part of the educational process (remember, when somebody says no, what they really need is more information) so they can build value in someone's mind. When someone says "yes", we simply take their order or schedule them on our calendar. *When somebody says "no", that's when we begin to take advantage of the opportunity to build value.*

If you only make $20 a call off the "yes," then how much money did you make off the "no's?"

If you had nine "no's", 9 x $20 is $180.

So you made $20 off the yes and $180 *off the no's!*

It appears to me that the big money is really in the "no's"!

Let's take this same example and make it a bit more interesting.

What if you only needed *five* contacts to make a $200 profit? You'd make $40 per call instead of $20.

And what if you sold *more than normal* one day and made a $300 profit with the same five contacts? That's $60 per contact. It's starting to get interesting!

Then what if, one day, you made a $300 profit from just three contacts. That's $100 per call, even if they say "no!"

Now think about it. If you could make $100 every time you picked up the phone or made a sales contact, could you see yourself getting to the point where you didn't care what they said? And if $100 per call isn't enough to get you to pick up the phone or make a contact, how much money would you need?

It's definitely worth our time to increase our personal activity level and educate as many people as possible. You may be making $1000 or $5000 per call or more in your line of work. However, it only happens when you actually make the call or contact.

If you are paid extremely well when you call, how much do you make if you *don't* call?

Absolutely nothing.

Learning to overcome rejection and "falling in love with the no's" is simply the process whereby we learn to live with the necessary level of activity for us to produce the outcomes we want for our life and business.

Falling in love with the "no's" doesn't happen overnight. If you are patient, you begin to realize how essential the "no's" are to getting to "yes". You'll find they grow on you!

We simply need to persist. I think you'll be pleased to find the environment doesn't matter; if we hang in there, success is inevitable!

Where could you apply this principle? Where are you giving up too soon? What circumstances do you have that are hooking you into rejection, causing you to back off rather than push ahead? What is stopping you from accomplishing what you've been wanting to do?

BECOMING MORE CREATIVE

My tendency to back off prevented me from having success at an earlier stage in my career. Rejection was a barrier that I would eventually need to overcome if I was going to accomplish what I wanted in life. Redefining myself and attaching a monetary value to each contact I made were just a few of the ways I began to deal with rejection issues.

Although I graduated from college with a degree in sales from Memphis State, I've often been curious as to what could have possessed me to get involved in a business that required 30 cold calls a day with constant rejection, especially since my tendency was to shy away from rejection environments. What caused me to reject job offers that included a decent salary, car, expense account, etc?

I believe that there was something deep inside of me that said, "If you're going to have a chance to do what you're here to do, you need to figure out how to deal with rejection; you then will be required to develop the skills to overcome it once you have understood your predispositions and some of your early experiences. "If you don't deal with this, then you won't have the life that you're capable of having, because you ultimately will have settled for less only to avoid rejection."

I continued the process by becoming more creative as I went. After I realized I was making $20 per call, I took a 3 X 5 index card and wrote "*I'm earning $20 each time I pick up the phone and call, whether they say yes or no. And to be perfectly honest, I could care less what they say!*"

What was my reason for doing this? Because I cared too much what other people thought and said, and that wasn't serving my purpose for building my sales business. Yet I didn't stop there. I took it one step further. I got a crisp $20 bill (or whatever my per call average was at the time) and I taped it to the bottom of the 3 X 5 card so I could pay myself after each phone call.

I needed a tangible way to remind myself that even though the "no's" were the most difficult part of my selling responsibilities, in order *to get the results I wanted,* I needed to go through the process.

Today, as I travel around the country speaking and training, I often have sales people only half-jokingly say to me, " I'd do a lot better in my business, if someone would just book these appointments (or make these phone calls) for me!" Leaving ourselves open for rejection is the most challenging part of the sales process. We put our whole being on the line.

So, instead of waiting for compensation at the end of the selling cycle, it made sense to compensate myself at the moment I was doing my most challenging activity. This way, my mind and emotions didn't compromise my selling activity level.

I find that many people aren't successful in their own venture or business because they don't create an environment that's conducive to persistence towards the desired outcome. When we create this kind of environment for ourselves, we have a far better chance of producing ongoing results. Stop and think about it. When you collect the money, that's the point when you *complete* the process. If you have a per call average, you actually *make* the money when you make the calls!

THE NUMBERS GAME

We know that all businesses to some degree are a numbers game, influenced by our activity level.

Cavett Robert, one of the great public speakers of our time and founder of the National Speakers Association, once told this story:

A man in commission sales came to work one day to find an envelope on his desk. He opened it and saw a blue slip inside. He called his wife and said, "Honey, I think I got a raise! I'm opening the envelope now; they always send a blue slip when somebody gets a raise or an increase!" He pulled out the blue slip and read it to his wife. It said, *"Because you're working on straight commission, your raise becomes effective when you do!"*

Making large amounts of money is possible when we're in business for ourselves. The reality is that, if we make money on straight commission, how much we make is based on what we sell. The harsh reality is that if we don't keep the activity level up, the business stops coming in. Unfortunately, if you wait until you really need to make a sale, it's too late.

RESPONSIBLE WAYS TO PROTECT
OUR ACTIVITY LEVEL

No matter how gifted we are in sales, we can't effectively sell our product or service if we don't believe in it. Once we have taken the time to do our "due diligence" to find out about the company and what we are to sell, we want to be in a position of genuinely believing in the product. Even with the best of products, if we keep getting "no's", over and over again, we begin to question the credibility of our work and of our product line. Then, we wonder if somehow, there's a conflict with us or the product. We begin to question our ability to produce because we don't know if we're *really* providing a great service. If we're not careful, we can talk ourselves out of future business! We begin to feel our credibility is not as great as it could be. We need to protect ourselves against those thoughts and feelings.

Most of us know from personal experience that our mind can play tricks on us. It's going to be swayed by whatever comes up in the middle of an anxiety-filled situation where there's potential for rejection.

Here's good news! Your mind doesn't have to be filled with anxiety. It doesn't have to accept rejection!

WHAT TO TELL YOURSELF
WHEN YOU HEAR "NO"

What do you normally say when you hang up the phone after getting a "no"? It's not pleasant, is it? You may be tempted when you've just hung up the phone to sarcastically think to yourself, "Great. This is really working out; I'm setting the world on fire now. If I keep this up, I'll be out of business in no time!" The last thing we want to do is pick up the phone and make another call. Instead, you might think, "What I need is to fix myself a little snack and maybe have a double-sized cup of coffee to get my energy level back up. After I'm re-energized, I'll get back in there and hit that phone again."

Then you may go in the kitchen, open the refrigerator—letting all the cold air leak out—while you stand there staring ahead in a trance, memorizing the contents. Then on the way back to the phone after your "pick me up," you hear "Oprah" from the den saying, "Today we're going to be talking about my current weight loss success and how my success can happen for you. . . ."

You may think, "I'll just 'veg out' with Oprah."

The sad truth is as entertaining as Oprah may be, you are *not* making calls or money. You *are* watching people who are paid millions of dollars to provide "entertainment", which I believe serves as a numbing escape from reality, while you lose the opportunity to actually create the income and life you want for yourself in the real world. You know your own "Oprah Moment".

WAYS TO BEAT THE "NO" BLUES

To make sure you don't fall into this escape trap, here's something you may find encouraging. When you get a "no" and you hang up the phone, say to yourself, "Thanks for the $20 bucks!" See if you don't smile when you say this. . . especially when you say it out loud! Isn't this approach healthier and more encouraging than what we normally say to ourselves after hearing "no"?

LESSONS FROM A FRAM OIL COMMERCIAL

There was an old Fram oil filter commercial where a man comes on the screen and says, "*Here's your choice. You can pay me now or you'll pay me later. But sooner or later, you're gonna end up paying. . . because if you don't buy this oil filter now and your engine blows up or something happens, then you'll end up paying big time!*"

Every prospect is determining how much we believe in our product and service by how long we're willing to persist to reach them. I suggest when you hang up the phone, after you say "Thanks for the 20 bucks," smile and say to yourself:

"You can either buy now or you can buy later. However, sooner or later, you'll want to buy. *I'm not giving up.* I'll persist until you finally figure out that I'm serious about working with you. There's real value here and this can benefit you and serve you well."

If this is someone with whom you really want to do business, you're not going to give up. Challenge yourself to get creative. Eventually you'll get the outcome you want. Then, if you allow anything to get in the way of that momentum, you are allowing something besides yourself to determine what you think about your product and service. What you think and feel is something you predetermine and it won't change based on anyone else's response.

Remind yourself of the great feeling of satisfaction that comes when you know you have served a client well. Before you pick up the phone, remember how pleased he or she was with your service or product. *That one simple thought alone can do as much as anything else to prevent the rejection feeling from setting in.*

THE FIVE-STEP PROCESS

Here is a five-step process you can use to protect yourself from falling prey to potentially immobilizing rejection feelings:

1) Keep in touch with your prospect. Ask them, "*Is it okay if I keep in touch to let you know when there's something new you might be interested in?*"

They may say "yes" and you end your conversation with a "yes" answer—leaving you open for another yes answer in the future. A "not yet" is definitely better than a "no!" If you follow through and keep in contact with them every month or two, after three to five phone calls, they might develop a curiosity about your business and allow you to gradually educate them with new information.

2) Determine your average sale and the average number of calls or contacts needed to produce it. For instance, your typical sale is $200. If you haven't figured out your average yet, first, monitor your sales over the next 30 days. Establish your average sale by taking the number of presentations you make and divide that number into your total sales for the 30-day period. This will give you your average sale per presentation Then, divide the number of contacts you made to produce those presentations or appointments into the number of presentations for the month. This will give you your current average sale and the average number of contacts it took to produce the sale. For instance, 10 calls produced a $200 sale. Each call is worth $20.

3) Make a 3 X 5 card and write the following: "I'm earning $20 (or whatever the amount) each time I pick up the phone whether they say yes or no." And then write, "To be perfectly honest, I could care less what you choose to answer!"

Do we care? Of course we do! That's the challenge. We often care too much what people say or think. When we think it through, it truly doesn't make any difference what they say! That's their business. Our business is to give them the chance to say yes, no, or maybe.

If they say yes, you help them with a product or service, or schedule an appointment.

If they say no, they simply need more. . .information!

Then you begin the process of educating them if you're committed to your business long term.

4) Take a fresh, crisp $20 bill and attach it to the bottom of the 3 x 5 card. Use it as a reminder of what your focus is, say "Thanks for the $20 bucks. You can either buy now or buy later, However, sooner or later you're going to want to buy." Then read the card. "I'm earning $20 each time I pick up the phone whether they say yes or no and to be honest, I don't really care what they say since my job is to keep making contacts and let the yeses come up as they may!"

5) Pick up the phone and make another call! Since it doesn't make any difference whether they say yes or no, it seems likely you could make more phone calls and more contacts. Realize that you get paid when you make the call and that's when you do the toughest part.

We really do the selling when we pick up the phone. Receiving the check is not making the sale; it is collecting the money from a sale you have already made. So, make sure you get reinforcement where you need it! Your 3 x 5 card can become your prospecting "best friend!" Now, feelings of rejection will never be the same! Now be honest, aren't you beginning to like those no's a little more already?

BE CAREFUL WHAT YOU SAY TO YOURSELF

What you say to yourself matters. Your internal dialogue, the thoughts and feelings you create, will help protect you mentally and emotionally from the downside of rejection—especially when you most need an effective activity level. When we do not deal with feelings of rejection we are unable to focus on the things we are capable of doing.

Anything that immobilizes us is a potential barrier that could eventually put us out of business. Once we have some protection like "Thanks for the $20 bucks!" and "You can pay me now or you can pay me later, I could care less", it becomes easier for us to take action. We can then make the contacts, share our story, give people a chance to participate, and at the least determine their current interest level. We can follow up appropriately by keeping in contact with them from time to time. One layer at a time, we educate them until they see the value and want to do business.

Now that we have a process, let's see what it looks like in action.

PROFESSIONAL PERSISTENCE

One day, I picked up the phone. It was a man who introduced himself as Lee Zachary. He said he worked for a financial services company and that he wanted to find out if I had a need for any additional financial services.

I asked him, "Lee, does this have anything to do with insurance?"

He said, "No, not exactly, although insurance is one of our products, that's not all we do."

I thought to myself, *"The last thing I need is more insurance."* So I replied, in a very nice voice, "If it's insurance, I don't need anymore!"

Lee said, "Well, if you don't need insurance, then what is it you need as far as financial services are concerned?"

I thought that was an excellent question, so I told him I needed more information about retirement accounts and college funds in order to set aside money for my children's education. "I need to know how much to put away."

He said, "I've got a questionnaire that will produce a computer printout that will give you the information you need. If I could provide this information for you, would you be willing to get together?"

I replied, "Yes, actually, it sounds like valuable information. I would like to know about those things."

"Well, Bill, when could we get together?" Lee asked.

"I don't know, it's probably going to be at least three weeks."

"I'll be in touch with you in about three weeks, then."

Three weeks came and went. Lee called me promptly when he said he would. (Don't you hate it when professional sales people do that!) He asked, "Can I come over and get some information?"

"Actually, Lee, now is not really the best time. . . ."

He said, "No problem, if now isn't the best time, when would be a better time?"

I told him in a couple more weeks.

Well, the long and short of it is, given my travel calendar, we played schedule "tag" trying to get together for about six weeks! And each time he simply inquired, "If now is not the time, when would be a better time?"

Finally, he asked me, "Bill, what's preventing us from getting together? Have you changed your mind about wanting more information about these things?"

"No, I'm still interested. I guess I'm just not convinced I need to set the time aside now, when so many other things are pressing."

"Bill, if we could do this without imposing too much on your schedule, would you want to go ahead and do this now?" When I said yes, he went on, "I'll respect your time constraints. How much time could you give me without feeling uncomfortable?"

"Probably about 20 minutes would be *max.*"

"I can do that. If I promise that I'll stick to 20 minutes, would you feel comfortable with me coming over now?" I said yes and Lee came over and he did *exactly* what he said he would. He kept to 20 minutes.

When Lee was leaving, he said, "Thank you for letting me gather this information about you and your family, I'll be back in about ten days with the report."

After three or four more scheduling attempts, we got together again. Lee told me, "Based on what I've evaluated, I agree that you don't need any more insurance. However, to meet your objectives for investing properly for your retirement and college for your children, although you are pretty much on target now, you're going to need to pick up the pace and invest a little heavier at these particular benchmarks."

Lee pointed them out to me and showed what the progression needed to be. It was extremely helpful information. When he left, I told him, "I appreciate your hanging in there with me. This is information I really needed. I appreciate your persistence in getting together and I want to thank you for keeping your commitment to the time constraints."

Lee said, "You know, it's my privilege to serve you and I'd like to have your business as time goes by. Are you satisfied with the person who's providing your financial services?"

I said, "Yes." As he was leaving he asked, "Would it be okay with you if I kept in contact from time to time, just to make sure you have what you need?" I told him it would be fine. I really appreciated the helpful information he had provided and his professionalism.

About a week later, there was a knock at my front door. Lee Zachary was there and I thought that maybe I had missed an appointment, however he said, "No, actually, I can't stay. My wife's out in the car, we just wanted to stop by for a moment and drop by this book. We found it quite helpful and thought you and Kay would enjoy it."

At the time my wife, Kay, and I were expecting our first child. Lee handed me the book *The First Twelve Months*. This book became Kay's favorite and she began reading it to me over breakfast.

A few weeks later Lee called and said, "Did you say you liked to play golf? We've got a tee time of 9:30 tomorrow and we need one more for a foursome. Would you be interested in joining us?" I love to play golf and gladly accepted his invitation. The next morning when I met him in the parking lot he told me the other two men had canceled. I thought, "Oh no, here it comes. So this is how you operate. You get me out on the golf course and then you have four hours to hammer me with your sales presentation!"

I was prepared for him to talk business and "hit me up," yet to my surprise he didn't bring up business at all! We got to know each other and found we had a lot in common.

As I was putting my clubs in the trunk, I thought to myself, "This guy's okay. I like the way he operates." I wished there was some way I could give him some of my business. I stopped and wondered, "Now, how did he get me to think that?" The answer is quite simple. He built a relationship that wasn't self serving, instead he served me with professional persistence.

Several weeks later, I called my financial planners to ask a question. They didn't return my calls. So, who did I call? You guessed it. I called Lee Zachary!

I told him, "You've given me better service without making any money than the person I've been working with. I'd like to switch my business over to you. Would you be willing to come over and set it up?"

Lee laughingly said, "Sure Bill, I'd be happy to come right over and I won't even make you wait!"

When we talked I told him how impressed I was with his tenacity. Lee said, "I made a decision when I started my business that I wanted to work with doctors, lawyers, CPAs, and self-employed entrepreneurs. You fit the entrepreneur category. I wanted to do business with you, so I gave you whatever time you needed to decide. The fact of the matter is, it really had nothing to do with you, it had to do with me and the decision I made about the kind of business and the kind of clientele I wanted to create. To be honest, you went early—some of my clients take two to three years!

What did Lee do that we can apply to our own approach? Can you see the excellent selling principles? I built my business on these same principles: "I believe enough in myself, my product and my service that I'm willing to build a relationship based on value, service and information. I knew that given the opportunity, if I did my part, there was the chance that you would see the value in us working together!"

Lee knew it was worth two to three years of persistence because the lifetime value of a customer is more than worth the up front effort! Like Lee, there are some clients that have taken me years to bring on board. However, I knew it was worth it to be patient and persevere because once I brought them on board, we would both benefit from the business relationship.

However, if I'm not able to overcome initial rejection, I'll never be able to have the long term, mutually beneficial relationships I want for my business.

BUILDING RELATIONSHIPS

Like Lee Zachary, do you believe that it's important to listen to what would benefit our clients and potential clients? If we care enough to get involved and be tangibly supportive, wouldn't people value working with us?

When other people show interest in you and care enough to really find out what you like, how you like to be treated, providing information and professional support, don't you want to give them your business?

There are creative ways of contacting people. You can send a sample, a note, and you can use the phone. A sales person can let people know gradually about the different products and services available, educating them about *their* company. Over time, you show them you know and care about *them*. When you genuinely care about their needs *first*, they will be interested in hearing what you have to say. Once you reach a certain point, *you* decide if their values, the way they operate and treat their people are acceptable to *you*. You decide who you work with.

I can't provide the high level of customer service and value I want to deliver if I'm trying to reach too many people. So, I've learned to be careful about whom I choose to work with. There are three questions that I believe can help establish rapport and begin building trust. These questions are designed to gather core information about an individual to help make a personal connection. You can start out by asking, "Would it be okay with you if I ask you a couple of questions, and find out a little about you and your needs before we begin to talk about specifics?"

We need to make sure we let them know that we want to find out who they are. Also, we want to find out what they might need most from our services.

1. "Would you tell me a little bit about yourself?" Or, if you know them you might ask, "Would you tell me a little bit about your current situation?"

Opened-ended questions of this sort help establish that you are not there to push your agenda, you genuinely want to find out about who they are and how to best meet their needs.

2. "What do you appreciate the most (and/or least) about your organization and what you do?"

By focusing on them, they quickly get the message that you really do want to meet their needs because you take the time to ask!

3. "If you could have the ideal work or career situation or the ideal outcome for you, what would that be?"

This gives you the opportunity to find out what's important to them.

At one of my seminars, I asked the participants to interview each other and ask the above questions. Here are some of the responses:

"I felt like I stopped selling to her as she was describing what was going on. I felt as if I had known her for months, although I had only known her for a few minutes. I visualized what she was about, and I felt like I could help her."

"I realized that I was listening more than I normally do, which leads me to believe I might be talking my prospects to death!"

"I found that I had more confidence about what I had to offer when I took just a couple of minutes on the front end to discover what they wanted."

Then I asked the group a question, how long did this exercise take? *Only two minutes.*

I then asked if they felt this exercise built some credibility, trust, and rapport. Their answer was a resounding, "Yes!"

It seems reasonable to challenge ourselves to take two minutes to connect with someone on a personal level before we ask them to trust us with their hard earned dollars or make a career change.

PREVENT SELLING MALPRACTICE

Picture yourself sitting in the waiting room at your doctor's office. The nurse calls your name and whisks you into an examination room where she takes your vital signs. Then she hands you one of those paper-thin gowns quite open and breezy in the back. You put it on, crawl up on the cold exam table (lined with a long strip of "butcher" paper) and let your feet dangle off the end waiting for the doctor to come in.

Finally, the doctor bursts in the room in his white lab coat with his name embroidered in cursive. He pushes his half glasses up on the bridge of his nose and begins to flip through your chart and the 14 forms you just filled out. He looks up and says, "I've been in medicine over 30 years and I've developed the uncanny ability to just look at my patients and make a diagnosis. From looking at you, I think you need a gall bladder operation. I'll schedule it on Thursday. Just talk to the receptionist when you go out and she'll give you all of the details."

This isn't how doctors normally operate! If they did, you'd probably want a second opinion! You expect someone to do a thorough examination, run some lab tests, and ask you exhaustive questions, listening to a history of your symptoms, maybe hit you a time or two with that little rubber hammer before they even think about surgery!

Tony Alessandra in his book *Non-Manipulative Selling* states, "In medicine and sales, making a diagnosis prior to an examination is malpractice!" The process of building trust and rapport with our potential clients is essential in determining what they need. Many times, we focus on ourselves and feel we need to prove to somebody we know what we are talking about. However, when we focus on them and their needs, we don't have to prove ourselves. *Listening* proves it for us.

In any case, establishing a personal connection is the best way to start off. They may quickly shift us to business and that's okay. If that's where they want to focus, we need to honor that. However, there are many people who, if we shift gears into business too quickly, might be offended thinking we are only interested in selling to them.

You can easily begin establishing rapport with one simple question, "Tell me a little about yourself or your current situation." Many times, that is enough. You may not even need to use the other questions, however you have three questions prepared just in case you need them.

SUPERLATIVE "MR. SPENCE" SERVICE

When I was in college, back in the bell-bottom years, there was a clothing store in Memphis called James Davis & Sons that my fraternity brothers and I liked. There was an older gentleman who worked there; his name was Mr. Spence. He had brilliant, white hair. I think he had worked at the store since it opened in the 1940s. This store was a town landmark; James Davis & Sons was a traditional fine clothing store (on the expensive side for guys in college!) that catered to clothing for men and boys. The store had old wooden floors that gently creaked while you walked around. The store had a comfortable "old glove" feeling and I loved to go in and browse.

Whenever I walked in, Mr. Spence would come from the back of the store to greet me. He'd grab my hand with a hearty handshake and say, "Bill, Bill, it's great to see you, I've been waiting for you. I've got some things I've been holding to show you. I knew you'd be in."

Still holding on to my hand, he'd lead me to a large walnut table and begin to pull some shirts out of cubby holes. He'd spread the shirts out on the table and say, "I know you like these French cuff shirts and here are some others I know are your favorite style." He'd lay them out on the table and I always liked everything he picked out. Then he would grab a handful of ties and start tying those little knots and laying them out on the shirts.

He'd motion to Mr. Nedelkovich and say, "Mr. Ned, bring over those suits that I told you to hold for me, the gray one and the blue one, so Bill can see how great these shirts and ties look!" Although I wasn't shopping for suits, I was able to see the high quality of the shirts and ties against expensive, hand tailored suits.

Then Mr. Spence would look at me in a kind of grandfatherly, protective way, and ask me, "Son, how are you doing on your socks and your belts? You know we forget about those sometimes." I'd say, "Yes, sir. You're right about that."

Then he'd pull out a fine belt and say, "This belt is a Trafalgar, one of the finest belts made in England. It's made out of the finest harness leather and since it's double stitched, it won't come apart. Just look at this buckle; it's solid brass so it won't tarnish or flake like those inexpensive belts. This belt is a great value, Bill, and it will wear well. So when you're ready for a belt, you come see me."

When he was finished, I'd look at the tasteful, quality clothing he'd laid out and say, "Mr. Spence, I really like the shirts and ties you picked out, so for now, I'll take those."

There were times I would think it's going to take Mr. Spence at least 45 minutes to clean up the table full of clothes he laid out! Yet, he never seemed to mind or put pressure on me.

As I was walking out of the store, I looked back and thought, "I might as well buy that nice belt while I'm here since I know I need one anyway. If I buy a "junk" belt somewhere, more likely than not, it will wear out quickly and I'll end up having to buy another one. If I buy one that will last, I'll get my money's worth. I trust Mr. Spence. This will be money well spent."

This is the part I loved best about Mr. Spence! When I went back to buy the belt, Mr. Spence *questioned* me, "Are you sure you want to buy this now, Bill? You could always get it next time."

"Yes, sir. I'm not planning to be back for awhile, so I'll go ahead and get it now." Then I'd leave knowing that I'd invested my clothing dollars wisely.

I always liked the fact that Mr. Spence knew me, what I liked and what would be an excellent, long term investment of my money. More often than not, I'd leave with a bag full of clothes. Even on those occasions when I "stretched my budget" a little, I knew I was getting the best value and that Mr. Spence would help me make the smart decisions for the long run. Not surprisingly, I continued to buy from Mr. Spence for many years after college!

A number of years later, when I moved to Texas, one of the first things I did was to look for a similar clothing store with someone like Mr. Spence to service me. I found a store that looked like it carried the kind of classic clothes I liked.

One day, I walked in and there wasn't anyone around to wait on me other than a young man sitting on the floor putting stock on a shelf.

I waited for a minute, then I said, "Excuse me, I hate to interrupt your work, could I get some help with these shirts?" I'll bet you've been in this situation before and you know what's coming. . . .The young man looked up at me and said, "Yeah, sure, if you can wait just a second, I'll be finished."

When he finally came over, I inquired about a particular cotton shirt. The young man said, "Well, we carry them, but we're out." I asked if he would take my credit card and mail it to me when it came in. He agreed and did the paperwork. Guess what? He never called me to say the shirts were in, never processed my credit card and I never heard from him again! My calls to the store were to no avail. Nobody had any idea what had happened.

This wasn't the kind of service I'd grown accustomed to from Mr. Spence, so I called him, saying, "Mr. Spence, I can't get anybody to sell me anything down here."

Mr. Spence said, "Bill, you know I'll take care of you. What do you need? Tell me what you want and I'll mail it right away. I'll pay for shipping. You know we want to keep your business!" Mr. Spence always kept his word. He took excellent care of me as a customer and I did business with him until he retired.

THE POWER OF REFERRAL ADVERTISING

All of us are looking to work with someone who will provide professional service. When we find them, we give them all of our business as well as refer other people to them.

One day a woman came to my front door and handed me her business card and a beautiful, fresh organically grown apple. She introduced herself as the owner of a new business called, "Farmer Fresh," and under the name it said, "Dirt to Door." She asked me if my family would prefer natural, fresh fruit and vegetables to the ones that were "vine ripened" with gas and chemicals. I said yes, however it wasn't easy to take the time to go into Dallas to shop at the Farmers Market.

She explained that this was a common problem and that other people had the same kinds of difficulties getting healthy produce for their families. So, she started a small business where she would truck in organic, natural produce directly from the field into neighborhoods, hence the name "Dirt to Door."

She invited me out to her truck where she had a beautiful assortment of fruits and vegetables. She told me she would call me on Monday evening to see what I wanted and leave my order at my doorstep—all I had to do was leave a check at the door!

I really appreciated how easy this was and I asked her how she got started.

"I found my children became healthier when they began eating natural fruits and vegetables that were high in distilled water and enriching enzymes. When we ate these healthy foods, and gradually weaned ourselves from junk food with lots of additives and processed snack foods, we all became healthier."

"Because we had such a busy lifestyle, it became difficult to always get what we needed. I figured, there are probably other families like mine who wanted to eat healthy and it wasn't convenient for them. So I decided to provide a service that made it easy for them and their families. . .and here I am!"

I was both impressed and appreciative of her efforts. Kay and I had recently discussed how we wanted our girls' to eat healthier foods. However, with my traveling schedule and the girls various activities, it was almost impossible to make the trips to the specialty health food stores. I immediately signed up for her service!

I then asked her how her business was doing and if she would like more business. Her answer was a quick, "Yes!" I really wanted her to be successful and ensure that she was able to continue providing this wonderful service!

I ran into the house, grabbed my cell phone and called a few of my neighbors. "John, does your family like fresh fruits and vegetables straight from the garden? Great. I want you to meet someone and I'm sending her right over. She's got a great service that I think you would be interested in!"

Before she left, my neighbor pulled up in her driveway and I went over to her car and introduced the produce lady. My neighbor was thrilled with what she had to offer!

I told the produce lady that if she needed any more names, I'd be happy to give them to her because I wanted what she had to offer.

The next week, along with my order, I found a sack full of beautiful, fresh tomatoes with a nice "thank you" note. I appreciated the courtesy. I sincerely wanted to help her do well in her business by spreading the word.

If we provide a valuable service that helps or contributes in some way, our customers will be appreciative and help get the word out. I'm pleased to say how well this has worked in my business since I rely heavily on referrals for new clients! It wasn't easy at first. It required my accepting responsibility for learning how to overcome rejection in order to get the word out so that I could build my clientele for long-term repeat business.

FOOD FOR THOUGHT

- What are your natural predispositions: outgoing, shy, healthy, chronically ill? How do they influence the direction you are taking?

- How have your seeds prepared you for your life direction?

- Are there seeds that have created challenges for you? If not rejection, what would your issues be?

- What personal responsibility would you need to take for better using your gifts and working through your early "seed" issues?

CHAPTER 2

Roots

I remember a story my mother told me about my childhood. She said I loved to talk. She related that when we went for walks, she would push me in the stroller and I would say "Hi, man" to everyone I saw. I was outgoing before I could even walk and as soon as I could talk, I was speaking to everyone. Today I talk for a living. When I was a child I talked because it met my need for attention.

Everybody does not necessarily know how to meet their own needs, yet we do the best we can! Maybe we get what we need from our parents, or from another source such as grandparents, aunts, uncles, brothers or sisters. We are continually trying to meet our needs. In the first six or seven years of life, our seeds begin to take root. This creates a foundation on which we begin to make decisions.

Our "root system" is an important part of who we become later in life. Is it okay to be who we are, or do we need to be somebody different? Is what we say or what we do acceptable? Is our family trying to change us? Would they prefer that we had been a boy if we are a girl, or a girl if we are a boy? Is the message telling us to be smarter, faster, bigger?

What kinds of messages enhance our chances to be healthy and go our own way? Are there issues we need to work through when we begin to make decisions about ourselves?

THE CHINESE BAMBOO TREE

When the Chinese bamboo tree seed is planted, nothing happens. There's no sprout for the first year. You water, fertilize and weed, still nothing happens. Even in the second, third and fourth years, nothing happens. Finally, in the middle of the fifth year, there's a sprout.

Then, within six weeks the Chinese bamboo tree grows ninety feet!

What was it doing during all those years? On the surface it may have appeared that nothing was happening, however the tree used that time to develop a root system.

If a ninety-foot tree needs four and a half years of roots to sustain it, how capable are we of growing to our full potential based on the roots we have? How high can our tree grow? And how do we develop the root system we have? How have environmental factors influenced us? Have they created doubts or fears that we need to acknowledge or work through? How comfortable are we with who we actually are?

We've all heard stories of people who begin to have flashbacks of abuse—whether sexual, physical or emotional—that they have previously been unable to recall. They suddenly realize the reason they have barriers that prohibit them from having healthy relationships. In this situation, the impact of early environmental influences (or roots) is apparent.

Other situations may not be as clear. There may be subtle "roots" that tell us that we can't do the things we want to because our environment is more powerful than we are.

These roots may have been formed by parents, babysitters, nannies, preschool teachers, church, or school environments. Roots can also form during other experiences from childhood such as team sports or even an illness. Roots can also be affected by some significant event that fosters a lack of belief in ourselves as opposed to a belief that we can overcome our circumstances.

TAKING RESPONSIBILITY FOR OUR DIRECTION

James Allen, who wrote *As A Man Thinketh*, states, "Let failure find its false content in that poor word 'environment.'"

When I was a kid my root issue was a need for attention. I needed to be the life of the party because I wanted affection and recognition. As an only child for the first few years of my life, it was heaven being the center of attention. I wanted to perform so I was very verbal. Looking back, I realize I wanted my world to be a friendlier place. I probably needed attention, nurturing and affirmation to counterbalance my environment. Fortunately my parents and extended family provided much of what I needed.

Did my early environment mean I was doomed to an unsuccessful life from the start? Absolutely not! The older I become, the more thankful I am that my general environment was so healthy. My natural abilities, in addition to learning persistence during challenging situations, have been invaluable in shaping my chosen direction along the way.

Looking at what has happened in the past teaches us about the influences or roots that exist and gives us the opportunity to change. It is critical to understand that this message is about hope! A teacher once told me, "You can survive about forty days without food, four days in the desert without water, and only four minutes without hope."

The past does not have to control us. We may not be able to change what has happened in the past, We can influence what happens in the present and in the future by taking responsibility for the hindrances that may be blocking us from finding our own personal direction. We can put aside old patterns which prevent us from accomplishing what God has in store for our lives. Then we become free to use our unique gifts and talents.

Fortunately, we can relay these messages to ourselves now. The great news is that, as we become healthy, we can teach and affirm our children and provide them with healthy messages.

Many of us first experienced failure in our early environments. There may have been circumstances over which we had no control and were unable to influence. Obviously, we had a limited awareness and understanding of the situations we encountered. We didn't know exactly what to do, although we did the best we could. A part of maturity is the ability to develop coping mechanisms for dealing with complex, environmental influences and learning that we can overcome our circumstances. Developing effective coping mechanisms comes later. Early in life, we do whatever we can for "survival."

Some children develop a desire to please or a desire for perfectionism as they learn to follow the rules. Some children entertain or become class clowns and some become caretakers. These are ways that children receive attention at an early age.

What responsibility did you feel at an early age? What role do you play in your family? Birth order, as well as the behavioral tendencies of your parents, could possibly have had an influence on you. How do your parents operate? Are they fast or slow, task or relationship oriented, happy or unhappy? Do they get along, yell and scream, or give each other the silent treatment? Is there financial stress? What is their personal history? Are they working through their own issues?

We pick up on the overall message through the feelings we sense. These sensations translate into tension and insecurity, or confidence and creativity. If there is fighting, we feel fear; if there is support, we feel secure. Our environment shapes us. Instead of being stuck in the past, we have the opportunity now to make correct choices for ourselves rather than be controlled by early environmental influences.

If we're aware of the early roots and the environmental factors that influenced us, we can take steps to accept responsibility now.

There are things we choose to align ourselves with such as our beliefs and values, standards and priorities and things we deem important and choose to support. This is not about blame or being a victim. Quite the contrary.

Many baby boomers are beginning to deal with these kinds of issues in their 30s, 40s, and 50s. In the past, painful issues were shamefully hidden, turned inward with guilt. Now, TV is full of people baring the details of their lives and their past, looking for someone to blame. This isn't to say that these people haven't been hurt in truly dysfunctional families or situations, however blame doesn't take you forward. Though it seems unimaginable that an authority figure could ever betray the trust of a child, it does happen and it needs to be addressed. It's never too late to deal with root issues!

As we develop abilities and coping mechanisms, we come to a place where we can address our significant "root" issues. We have enough preparation or maturity to entertain thoughts that were either too painful or that we were unable to deal with before. Even though we may not have known what to do then, we know what to do now and we can accept responsibility for changing and learning from those issues in order to move on to a better place. Let's explore how our early environment may have set the stage for our development.

LEFT AND RIGHT-BRAIN DIFFERENCE

In 1961, Roger Sperry introduced the concept of left or right-brain dominance. His research indicated that each part of the brain governed a different aspect of activity in our thought processes, behavior and learning style. Researchers noted that, although there was more collaboration between the two hemispheres than originally reported, each side dominantly controlled specific functions. Although we draw on both left and right-brain hemispheres, we do have a preference for how we process information and how we approach our environment.

Left hemisphere functions include logic, details, analysis, step-by-step processes, language and mathematics. Left-brained people might become accountants, computer programmers or financial analysts. The right hemisphere of the brain governs things such as emotion, humor, dreams, physical movement, music, insight and intuition. Right-brained people might become artists, poets, fashion models or entertainers.

A close friend, Neli, recently had a stroke on the left side of her brain. Her right side is paralyzed and responding to physical therapy. Neli is from Brazil and Portuguese is her first language. It is interesting to note that her speech is gradually returning in Portuguese, more than in English. She has progressed to a point where she speaks a mixture of both languages yet doesn't know which language will come out when she speaks. Her incredible faith and indomitable spirit coupled with her supportive husband Bill are the keys to her progress. Through recovery she is finding a new direction for her life. Neli's recovery is an example of a left-brain dominant injury.

Even though every person has both left and right-brain abilities, one hemisphere will be predominant. When I refer to someone as being left-brained or right-brained, I mean someone who learns to function predominantly in that hemisphere of the brain.

The left side of the brain controls the right side of the body and the right side of the brain controls the left side of the body! Experts report that left-handed people are actually the only ones in their "right" mind. (Of course being a left-handed person myself, I've always felt there was some truth to this!)

Documented cases of hemispherectomies do exist. In one case, the entire right hemisphere was removed and the patient survived with their left-brain speech function intact. However, they suffered from chronic depression and mood swings.

Dr. Rita Dunn at St. John's University has conducted extensive research on learning styles. Two primary designations of learning influences are analytical and global. These correspond with the left-brain and right-brain. She teaches that left-brain/analytical prefer learning environments with warm temperatures, bright lighting, a formal structured format and learning from a credentialed expert. They prefer to stay in one place and not move around. They do not want to eat or drink anything because they find it distracting. Dr. Dunn defines this style as "low mobility-low intake."

Right-brain/global on the other hand, prefer learning environments with cool temperatures, dim lighting, music in the background, informal, unstructured settings like bean-bag chairs or sitting on the floor. They prefer to learn by doing and personal experience rather than learning from books and manuals. They like to move around and have food and drink readily available. She defines this style as "high mobility-high intake."

Most people draw from both learning styles with a primary emphasis on one or the other.

Dr. Dunn also identifies the sequence of learning that complements each style. For example, some people may learn best visually, first seeing the information written in a book, on a chalkboard or chart. Other people are auditory, learning best by hearing the information first on a tape or in a lecture. Babies, for example, are kinesthetic, they learn by doing. They'll pull up in their cribs over and over again until they learn through practice and repetition. Some people are tactile. They learn by drawing a model or writing an outline in their own words.

The sequence determines how easy or difficult the learning process is for each individual. This information can help you determine your optimum learning environment, causing you to perform at your top productivity while minimizing distractions. You will know how to create an environment that maximizes your learning potential.

Dr. Dunn's Learning Preference Inventory can help you determine your best sequence and preferred learning environment.

Environment has an impact on whether we are more right-brained or left-brained. Let's say there is a primarily "left-brained" child who was raised in a left-brained home. He comes home with his school papers and hands them to a parent, who says, "Put your papers in the "school file" and we'll look at them after your snack. Hang up your jacket on the peg marked with your name, put away your hat on the shelf and your mittens in the bin labeled 'accessories.' Change from school clothes into play clothes and put your school clothes in the hamper. Put your homework on your desk where you can work on it at 6:45 when it is time to do homework. Then wash your hands and come down for a snack. I'll have it prepared by then." This family lives with rules, guidelines and expectations that the child will learn to follow. It is environmental influence.

Across town there's a "right-brained" child growing up in a right-brained environment. She comes home from school with her school papers and her parent says, "Put your papers on the school pile next to the refrigerator. Honey, where are your papers? It's okay, I'll ask your teacher about them tomorrow. Throw your things in the closet, just get them out of sight. Go upstairs and see if you can dig up some clean things to play in out of the pile. There's clean laundry on the bed in my room and your play clothes are there. Did you ever find your book for your book report tomorrow? Do they let you use Cliff notes in the third grade? Don't worry, we'll come up with something." This child learns to live in an unstructured environment that isn't focused on rules, regulations, or external expectations.

HOW WE GROW UP

Growing up, I had a friend named Mark Wilson. One day Mark invited me over to play at his house. When we reached his back door he said, "Oh yeah, take your shoes off." Not only had shoes never touched the carpet of the Wilson home, human feet had never touched the carpet. There were plastic runners going from room to room.

When we tried to find a place to play, Mark's mother told us we could play in the house if we stayed on the kitchen floor. There wasn't much to do in there so we snuck into the dining room while his mother was doing some heavy cleaning. We made a fort with a couple of blankets draped over the table and were having a great time in our new creation when Mrs. Wilson came in.

"Mark, you and your friend get out from under there! Look what you did to my table. You're going to clean off all those fingerprints right now, young man. You take your friend and go outside to play. I work hard to keep a clean house for you and your father. You go play somewhere else."

I felt sad for Mark. "Let's go to my house and play." As we left I asked him, "Is your house like that all the time? You can't even live in it, much less have fun."

After we played at my house, he said, "I had more fun today than I've ever had at home." I don't know if there is any connection or not, however a year after we moved away from there, my mother told me Mark's father had died of a heart attack. He was only 42 years old and a banker.

The right-brained child may not even make it home. They might get sidetracked chasing a squirrel or begin playing with friends. The child doesn't bring the test home from school because they forgot. And if they do bring it home, it may be wadded up, torn or covered with mud. They may even try to hide it from their parents because of the low grade. They forgot to study because they were having such a great time the night before. And if they did study, they either didn't take the time to understand it or because they decided it was boring, didn't discipline themselves to study. When they finally make it home, they stick their little fist up with their paper wrapped around it. Their parent unravels the test paper and says, "68%! Hon, couldn't you have done better than a 68%? I know you're smarter than that."

Then their precious prodigy bursts into tears and says, "I hate school. My teacher hates me, the kids hate me and I don't ever want to go back." The parent feels compassion and, instead of reading the child the riot act, they say, "Honey, I hate to see you upset like this. You know your father and I weren't too great in math either, we learned a long time ago that it's not what you know that determines whether or not you're going to be success-ful, it's who you know. You go out and play and have some fun with your friends. When you finish playing, bring your nice friends back and we'll pop some popcorn, make some Kool-Aid and play some games. Honey, you'll soon forget about this and we know you'll do better next time."

If you were to drive by a left-brained home, you might find a "YARD OF THE MONTH" sign out front. You'd probably see a guy after work walking around, hunting for weeds! He might have a little tool especially designed for digging up weeds. You would see him carefully kneel in the perfect grass and surgically remove the weed. He would then walk briskly into his garage/workshop where he had all of his tools neatly arranged on a peg-board in alphabetical order. He would then shake the loose dirt off the roots of the weed, take down a specially designed weed disposal bag and dispose of it properly!

Chances are the right-brainer doesn't even have a yard, let alone do yardwork. They believe that's the reason God invented condos! If you live in a condo, they do all that for you! This leaves the right-brainer more time to socialize. If they do have a yard, they don't have any grass, only a few bicycles in the dirt! They might also have a tree swing, slip and slide, yard darts and half the family silverware out front where you can find it.

They could also have a little Evel Knievel jump ramp out on the sidewalk where the neighborhood kids congregate to try their latest daredevil stunts. Those kids don't tell their parents what they are doing because they don't want to take a chance on losing the only decent place they have to really play.

The left-brainer grows up in a left-brained environment believing that if they make a mistake their acceptance might be in jeopardy. The right-brainer grows up in an environment that teaches that mistakes are okay and order is not what is important. What matters are relationships and connections. So the die is cast and the environmental influences are set.

I don't understand how God, in His infinite wisdom, allows a left-brained person to marry a right-brained person! The left-brained person would say to the right-brained person, "If it's the last thing I do, I'm going to help you get your act together. You're always scattered and you're never organized." You would leave your head somewhere if it wasn't attached to your shoulders. The right-brainer says, "If it's the last thing I do I'm going to help you loosen up and have a fun time! Quit being so compulsive. Don't sweat the small stuff (and by the way, everything's small stuff!)." So the conflict begins!

We not only battle it out with each other, but also with ourselves. Internally, we have one primary influence against the other. While drawing from both sides of the brain, we're either right-brain dominant or left-brain dominant. Let's say my goal is to be the best at what I do and be very successful. While I'm dreaming about that, my left-brain jumps in and says, "If that's ever going to become a reality, there are 987,463 synchronized step-by-step details you'll have to do." Then the right-brain says, "Don't tell me those things. I just wanted to think about it for a while." The left and the right begin to be in contention with each other.

A reason that the left-brain or the right-brain is more developed could be because of our early environment. We are comfortable with what is familiar. Left-brainers can't make spontaneous adjustment because it's too threatening. A right-brainer can't come home and tell their left-brained spouse, "Surprise, honey, we're going on vacation this weekend." That's not a left-brained person's idea of a joke! The left-brainer might say, "You don't mean this weekend? If we're going out of town, I'd have to put the dog in the kennel, pick up the cleaning, get my hair cut. You know that if we're going to do something like that I need four or five weeks lead time or it's just not worth doing. There's no way we can go." The right-brained person loves spontaneity. They may consider it actually necessary for their own survival. If they don't have it, their environment becomes restrictive—you know, boring.

I once saw the following scene actually happen. A left-brained person was receiving a gift from a right-brained person for their 25th wedding anniversary. It was a diamond ring with 25 diamonds signifying the 25 years of marriage. The right-brainer got down on one knee, gave a little speech, and said to his wife, "Surprise Honey! Happy anniversary!"

The left-brainer said, "A ring? What did you get me a ring for? Honey, you knew I really wanted a new microwave." The right-brainer did indeed know she wanted a microwave, however right-brainers don't give gifts that people want. They give the gifts they want people to have because they have a need to give something exciting. They probably gave up long ago trying to please a left-brainer since they could never get it exactly like the left-brainer wanted anyway.

There are some things right-brainers are hoping the left-brainers don't find out about them. For instance, even though there are still a few months left in the year, they've already locked their keys in the car five or six times. The right-brainer even bought a little metal box to hide the key under the hood, yet they can't find the box! They spend one to three hours a day looking for the keys and glasses. Think about it, that would be an extra month every year if you would get organized.

Or the right-brainer doesn't want the left-brainer to know they were in the grocery store the other day with a full basket of groceries, got to the checkout, and the cashier said, "That will be $487.00." Suddenly, they realized they not only don't have the checkbook and they don't have their wallet, purse, or anything. Does that bother the right-brainer? No! They just turn to the eleven left-brainers standing in line behind them and say, "Can you believe that? I left everything at home and didn't bring anything with me." The left brainers say to themselves, "No, actually I don't think I can believe that; how can you come to the store without your things?" None of this phases the right-brainer who says to the left-brainers, "Excuse me, would you watch my basket? I'll be right back?"

That's not the whole story. The right-brainer hopes the left-brainer doesn't find out when they find their checkbook that it hasn't been balanced since 1968, if ever. The right-brainers found out a long time ago it was a lot easier to just open a new account! The left-brainers might ask "Can you really do that? Don't you have to balance your checkbook. Isn't it some kind of law? And if you don't balance your checkbook, how do you know how much money is in your account?" Then the right-brainer will say, "Oh, that's easy. Just call up the bank and they'll tell you. Do you mean to tell me you've been keeping track of all that yourself when right down the street the bank is handling it for you? Doesn't that seem like a duplication of effort?" The left-brainer is asking, "Can you do that?"

Right-brainers just don't understand the reason you need to waste time with all the hassle. The left-brainer leaves the conversation mumbling to themselves "Can you really do that?"

Right-brainers don't require everything to turn out because they're always forgetting things and getting in trouble. As a result, they always know how to get out of trouble! The left-brainers, on the other hand, require that everything always work out. Because they seldom find themselves in trouble, they don't know how to get out of trouble. The left-brainers can't get into trouble because they don't know how to get out.

PERSONALIZING YOUR PRESENTATIONS — LEFT TO RIGHT

A left-brained sales person walking into a group of primarily right-brained prospects for a presentation might think, "This room is not the way I requested it. Things are not set up properly and I know my manual says I'm supposed to do things a specific way. It may appear to him that the room is full of confusion. The prospects have their friends there and they're visiting with each other and not paying attention. The left-brainer might think, "I don't know if I need to continue the presentation. This isn't the way it says in the book."

A left-brained person in a right-brained environment may feel uncomfortable and unable to adapt to the situation. They may think, "If it's the last thing I do, I'm going to get these people settled down and I'm going to teach them a thing or two about my product or services." This could, indeed, be the last thing they do with those clients!

What they can learn to do is grit their teeth, reach way down and come up with a funny story or two, loosen up and have a good time. The important point is they need to do this on purpose. If they can't loosen up and enjoy the experience, they need to at least laugh when everyone else does. If they can't do that they need to leave them alone and let them have fun all by themselves because they'll sell more when they've created an environment that is conducive for their clients to do business with them.

Even when the left-brainer makes the adjustment, it may not feel comfortable. He may leave that presentation thinking, "I don't think anybody learned anything." Before he can get out the door, one of the right-brains will pounces on him and say, "This has been great! I really enjoyed it. I want to give you names of people you could do business with. Give me everything you've got!"

If the left-brainer isn't careful, they'll say something highly persuasive like, "Huh, wait a minute. You were the one who wasn't listening! You lost my literature, you lost your pen, you weren't paying attention to a word I was saying. In all honesty, I don't know if I can sell you this much of my product unless you're willing to do a follow-up presentation now!"

The fact of the matter is that right-brainers will buy, and you can't teach them anything! How come? Because they're not using everything they know now; and if you try to teach them new information they will feel guilty because that's just more information they're not using. They just want to enjoy the relationship with you and have fun! Right-brainers will reward you for enjoying the experience by buying whatever you have. There doesn't have to be a reason. The right-brainer has an impulse to buy because they enjoy the experience.

ADJUSTING RIGHT TO LEFT

Then, there's the flip side. What happens when you have a right-brain salesperson going into a room full of left-brained prospects? They are running a bit late as they make their long awaited entrance. When they walk in, there are people sitting at tables, elbow to elbow with their hands folded, waiting, because they came to this meeting to be educated on the chosen topic. The right-brainer barges in and says, "I'm so glad you came. I can't guarantee you'll learn anything however we're going to have a lot of fun! We're going to get to know each other and this is going to be great. You're going to leave here really excited!"

The right-brainer can not only leap tall buildings in a single bound, they can introduce themselves to everybody at the table in 45 seconds or less and connect with everybody at the same time. The right-brainer is saying to himself, "I'll bet they wonder how I do it. I'll bet they would like to be a little bit more like me." The truth is that the left-brainers are saying to themselves, "Who are they? They're not the presenter, are they? I thought this was going to be an educational presentation and we were going to learn about this topic. This looks like it's going to be some kind of a free-for-all. This is not what I came for."

Then the right-brainer complicates things by thinking, "If it's the last thing I do, I'm going to get them to loosen up and have a good time." In fact, this may be the last thing they do for this client! The left-brained clients came for new information.

Many times, at this point, right-brainers feel the need to overcompensate for the lack of structure, so they'll say something to impress the client like, "We've got this great flip chart—I'll have to bring it next time", or "There's some great information that will allow this to make more sense. I don't have it with me right now, I'll get it to you when I find it." This is about as close to an educational process as they can come up with, without choosing to adjust their approach. One of the most difficult things the right-brainer will have to do is to give specific, detail oriented information. He's going to have to clench his fists, grit his teeth, and try to come up with something that resembles an educational process.

After he's finished his "class", the right-brainer may say to himself, "I'm out of here. This has been no fun for me. I don't care if anybody buys or not if I can't enjoy my work." The left-brainer may walk up as the right-brainer is storming out (feeling frustrated) and say, "Excuse me, before you go I'd like to say that I thought your presentation was very interesting. I've been looking for a system to deal with this area of my life and I like the way your product or service is organized into a system." (The left-brainer has a system for everything else in his life, such as getting his children off to school, organizing his wardrobe, taking care of his business and finances.)

The right-brainer replies, "You thought this was interesting? That's really funny. I've got to go." The left-brainer says, "Well, before you go I just want you to know that I don't want to go overboard or anything, however I'd at least like to get started with the your basic system." Because of the emotional turmoil the right-brainer feels after suffering through their presentation, if he's not careful, he'll say, "No, I'm not selling you anything because this has been no fun for me and it's not worth going through all this for one basic system." The truth of the matter is, right-brainers don't really care if they sell anything. They just want to have a fun time and enjoy the experience!

We need to have flexibility to approach our business with both in mind. What has to happen to cause us to choose to move beyond our initial environmental influence?

Cavett Robert tells the story of a senior surgeon at the Mayo Clinic who was addressing 900 new interns. The surgeon told his interns, "The human body is so incredible that nine times out of ten, it will heal itself if you don't do something to it to kill it!" We need to focus on how to prevent ourselves from killing our business simply by learning how to be flexible with people who think differently than we do.

A woman came to me with a story about how she had spent 23 years of married life trying to change her husband. When I asked her how it turned out, she told me they had gone through a divorce. She said, "He just wasn't the man I married anymore." In our zeal to remold another person, we wind up destroying some of the characteristics or qualities that attracted us to that person in the first place. What if our compatibility with other people is based on our willingness to accept their differences?

Remember that we're not just left-brained or right-brained. We're both! To be the most creative person we can be, we want to utilize both. We need to be willing to acknowledge the influence of our roots. Regardless of what our environment and background was we can accept how they are affecting us now. Acknowledgment functions as the beginning of confronting these issues to bring about change.

How do we apply these concepts in business? When looking at your ability to move forward, there are things you are doing well and things you are not doing well. When you go into business for yourself, you're required to do both left-brained and right-brained functions for your business to prosper whether you are naturally inclined that way or not! You need to make the sales calls and be persuasive yet you also need to write the checks, pay the bills and balance the books. Can you do it all?

What if you only build your business using your primary side? If you're left-brained, the outcome would be that you'd be highly structured however you'd have no business. If you're right-brained, you'd have plenty of business initially, yet you wouldn't follow up and customers would leave. Either way, you wouldn't have a business for long!

It's imperative we use both the left-brained and right-brained functions. We need to realize that if we have a tendency to do one or the other we have a responsibility to make adjustments and work through our discomfort. This truly is a brain-dominance issue. It's helpful to determine whether you're predominantly one way in order to integrate your less developed areas, making them more balanced. It's not natural or comfortable, however it can be a learned behavior for the purpose of producing the results we're after once we find our whole-brained direction.

SOUL'S JOURNEY

My soul's on her trip today
It can't decide whether to drive the slow trip the
thought provoking way
When the soul has time to contemplate, observe its
place in the scheme of things

Or to fly the fast and more expedient way
Requiring not the harsh reality of the day
Thus allowing more time to keep the numbing pace
More time when arrived at this trip's destination
To escape the tortured expectation of performance
By joining in a competitive game to play.

A dollar a hole winner buys
No rest for the weary soul in this
The body says more time for me this way.
The soul wins out this day

We'll drive starting early the slow unrushed trip by ground.
The low burn of spinning tires sing a prayerful mantra song.
Disengage they say
From where these expectations flow
Our growth is slow urged on by no less than commitment
to this thought.

Quiet prayerful reflection is then sustained by the
inner stretching out of the tortoise pace
The temptation still to pull up the buttercups in spring
To see how deep the root has grown so far.
To harvest that splendid yellow crop just prior to the
tender blooms unfolding wide.
Don't do it our soul cries out.
Yet we rush ahead to be there a bit too soon.

Don't help that bird out of it's shell
My grandfather would say to me
but wanting to help, I disobeyed.

It died, he said, because it needed the struggle to
finish the lungs and wings to breathe and fly
You tried to help your baby soul to fly too soon,
Now it's not strong enough to survive the life you've
chosen for it to lead.

The lessons then in the Chinese bamboo standing tall,
90 feet or so fully grown has an odd way of getting there,
for the first four years, nothing but seed beneath the soil
The fifth year is different though as the shoot begins
to uncoil above the earth
A six week trip to its full height, 90 feet or so.

How can this be all this time nothing to see
For this is the way a soul grows, mostly inside
Quietly waiting for that moment when preparation
meets opportunity to weather a life experience with
soul's roots deep and wide
to anchor firmly its towering tree trunk mast.
This is the soul's growth, not a passing lesson
but one that lasts.
My soul finally turns the blaring radio off
The prayerful hum is joined by rushing wind
A force to forever push against
But also listen to.

Its hushing tone, its pounding breath
Gives voice to our soul's whispering song
Don't rush along, be still
and know, no, remember, that I am here.

Bill Cantrell

FOOD FOR THOUGHT

In the course of thinking about your roots, you may discover you've let your direction be set by past events. You may discover you've not accepted the responsibility to go your own direction. You may find you are still being governed by early life experiences. You may even discover how something in your past triggers the choices you've been making and continue to make today.

How does somebody know if they're going the way that they need to go? You'll know it by whether or not you feel "congruent" now and whether it resonates inside with what your heart is telling you to do. You know if you've become another person just to please someone else.

Here are some questions to help you think about what significant issues you may have:

- How did your environment shape you?

- How did you learn to respond to your early environment?

- What was your birth order?

- How did your roots prepare you for what you're doing now?

- Does your life reflect who you are inside, or are you living a lie or wearing a mask?

- What roots and environmental influences did you have for which you now need to accept responsibility so you can move ahead?

CHAPTER 3

Trunk

Our experiences, environment, and early training prepare us to make life decisions that govern our understanding of our direction.

The model entitled "Personal History Transformations" will allow us to go through our entire life history to see what factors contribute to the direction we choose.

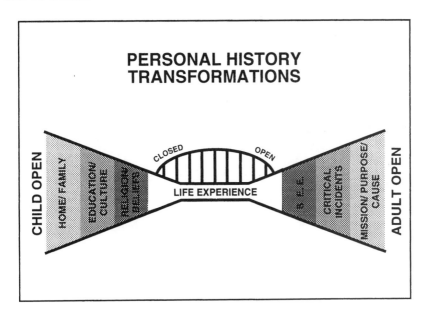

Child Open: When we are born, we are open and trusting. Most babies look directly into our eyes and receive love and affirmation from our gaze. A child grows through the teaching and other life-shaping factors the world provides.

Home and Family: This first environment sets our standards for what is normal and what is not. Our family builds our foundation for learning and growth. If our needs are not consistently met by the family, we will seek approval and support elsewhere. However, if the family is healthy, the nurturing they provide will be sufficient.

Education/Religion: These institutions influence us in our early development. They provide a formal structure to objectively evaluate ourselves in our intellectual and moral development.

Life Experience: This level represents the total life experiences to date that provide our current perception of life. We all have memories of supportive events as sources of encouragement. We also have challenging events in our history that might cause us to question our life's direction.

Significant Emotional Events (S.E.E.): These are life events that deeply impact our emotions. These sometimes move us to take action, or at the least, may cause us to pause and consider our life direction.

Critical Incident: This could be an automobile accident, winning the lottery, new relationship, health challenges, or a near death experience. A critical incident permanently changes our life. This is a turning point event in our life; in essence, a defining moment.

Mission Purpose Cause: These discoveries come out of our life experiences, significant emotional events, and life turning points. We discover what really gives our life meaning. Our mission constitutes our reason for living and a sense of purpose for our days in addition to the desire to make a valid contribution to our chosen cause.

Adult Open: This is the level of wisdom we reach. Hopefully, we become more accepting, tolerant, understanding, and flexible. We are able to grow from a narrow outlook to an open understanding that allows us to find our direction.

BEGINNINGS

Most children are curious about their new surroundings. Newborns are alert and responsive to their environment. They hunger and thirst for nurturing, love, acceptance, and physical closeness. Some children receive unconditional love and some do not. Based on the home and family we're born into, we may not realize how much we are influenced by this culture.

My story illustrates how the events and people in our life shape our direction as well as how to map a history using the "Personal Transformations" model.

My parents were my most influential teachers. My mother instilled in me her love for reading. My mother, primarily self-taught, studied all day long and taught class on Sundays. I always remember her sitting on the end of her couch, reading and studying her Bible. When I'd come in, she would share her new insights for the day with me. Besides being a teacher, my mother was also an example of how to relate to others. She is highly sensitive, displaying an almost sixth sense with people. She's always ready to help and she's at her absolute best in a crisis. I love her steadfast qualities.

I admire my father for starting his own business after years of working for corporations. He always dreamed of owning his own business and allowed me the privilege to be part of helping him grow. I think my father planted the seeds for my desire to, one day, have a business of my own. His honest, open and friendly manner, along with his fair and ethical business dealings have been my model from the beginning. I respect his ability to blend personal integrity with the ability to produce a lot of results.

Mary Louise Aste, my Latin and Greek teacher in high school, was another important teacher and mentor. Her classes helped me discipline myself to accomplish something I didn't think I could master. I was a "C" student, at best, and it was her faith in me that encouraged me to believe I could learn difficult subjects like latin and Greek. She would tell me, "Billy you may never be my smartest student, yet you'll be one of my favorites. You can learn this." My love for languages and word origins began with her influence. Through her passionate commitment to teaching, I began to enjoy mastering difficult concepts.

CAREER DECISIONS

I was involved in sports from the time I was five or six years old.

When I graduated from high school, I tried out for the Cincinnati Reds and the Oakland Athletics baseball teams. I was thrilled and honored to be trying out for professional ball. After tryouts, they told us that those of us who made the cuts would be contacted and informed of the next step. *Not* hearing from them was the way I knew I hadn't made it!

Playing professional baseball was my dream. Although I wasn't picked, I had to take the chance to take it as far as I could. Otherwise, I couldn't properly let go and move on. I've often thought how thankful I am to be where I am now. If I had made it in sports, I would have missed out on so much.

When I didn't make the team, I began to ask myself questions about how my early preparation affected my direction. "What am I going to do with my life? Am I going to go to work. Am I going to get a higher education, or both?" I decided to take some time off from school to work. My first real work experience became a turning point! I worked for two bricklayers named Shorty and Don Wright (the Wright brothers!) from Hernando, Mississippi. The Wright brothers discovered my middle name was Clyde. (I was named after my maternal grandfather who I'm sure was pleased to be named Clyde in the 20s. Clyde wasn't that popular in the 50s and 60s!). The bricklayers found out I was sensitive about the name Clyde, so immediately my nickname became Clyde. It was constantly "Clyde this" and "Clyde that."

One time they sent me out to the truck saying, "Fetch us a brick stretcher, Clyde." I held up every piece of equipment in the truck while they laughed, saying, "Nope, that's not it." It took a while before it dawned on me that I was on an initiation "snipe hunt!"

Their smirky way of taunting me bothered me. They would say, "Clyde, we know exactly what will happen if you go to college. You'll waste four long years of your life, then come crawling back to us begging for your old job back. And you know what we'll say? Forget it. You had your chance." According to them, I needed to learn bricklaying and work on their crew. They reasoned if I learned the trade and stuck with them, then one day I, too, could have a red Mustang 2+2 fastback and a double-wide trailer in one of the nicer trailer parks in Hernando, Mississippi.

At that time in my life, I have to admit I stopped and asked myself, "Is this really what I want out of life? Is this the direction I want to go?" However, I finally decided I was going to show the Wright brothers a thing or two. I was going to go to college, get an education and find out what I was supposed to do with my life. I knew I was tired of working twelve-hour days mixing cement and throwing bricks. I was convinced I needed to use my mind to develop my capacity. I wasn't going to give the Wright brothers the satisfaction of determining my direction, even though, in a way, they did just that.

It was at this point my father said, "Son, you've gone as far as you can with your baseball career. You know you don't want to work construction and there's something else out there for you. How about you come and let me teach you how to sell? It's been a nice profession for me. It's something

I think you'll enjoy doing plus I could use your help in my business."

So I worked for my father and attended Memphis State for my sales degree.

MY LIFE'S DIRECTION

Dr. Waylon Tonning was known as the Sales Doctor. He held the Sales chair at Memphis State University (the only University at the time with a credentialed major in Sales). Dr. Tonning continually amazed us with his knowledge, gained from selling for numerous companies.

He would walk in on the first day, ask a student where they grew up and, within a few questions, begin describing their neighborhood and the street name. Sometimes he would ask, "Did you grow up in that little red brick house on the corner?" We could hardly believe any one could have made that many calls to that many places. He *had* made that many calls, and I have always felt fortunate to have learned under him.

He told us that at that time only 2% of all college graduates got into sales and 1% of those were in family businesses. However, 5 years after graduation over 35% of all college graduates were in sales or marketing related fields.

In a Sales Training class in college, my professor (and now friend) Dr. Paul Green, the author of *Get Hired* , allowed me to research how the use of cassettes could effectively train sales people. Consequently, I listened to every Earl Nightingale tape program in the library (which was his entire tape library at the time). "The Strangest Secret" was the first motivational recording I had ever heard. I am only one of the millions influenced by Earl Nightingale's messages.

The Strangest Secret startled me with its alarming statistic. Nightingale pointed out that even though we live in the richest nation, less than 5% of all workers will have enough money to survive their retirement without social and family assistance if they retire at age 65. He challenged the listener to prepare for his or her lifetime. I was hooked. I couldn't get enough tapes to satisfy my insatiable thirst for this kind of inspirational information. This project was preparation for the next emotional event that occurred right before I graduated from Memphis State.

As an officer of Pi Sigma Epsilon, a sales and marketing fraternity, I had the opportunity to hear excellent speakers at the Local Sales and Marketing Executives International meeting. The speakers for the local meeting included Dave Yoho, Ty Boyd, and Don Hutson. I also attended the National Convention where a woman named Sandy Karn spoke on cause and effect. For me, it was a truly life changing lecture. When it was over, I asked her if I could help with her books and props. This gave me a chance to ask her about business principles. She was willing to sit down over a cup of tea, and give me further direction. Since that time, we have been friends and colleagues for twenty years.

I have always loved listening to my pastor and great men preach. I am often impressed as I listen to their messages and see them inspire people to change their lives. Though I knew the ministry was not the direction for my life, I loved the idea of inspiring people with a powerful message. My father was my early role model for a healthy, honest, integrative sales approach. I learned a great deal from my father's work, yet I also had a desire to help others grow through teaching spiritual, mental and emotional principles.

Sandy Karn's speech combined principles for both business and personal growth. I concluded, during her speech, that inspirational speaking, and sales training combined elements of preaching and teaching. It focuses on spiritual, mental and emotional concepts meant specifically for business and sales people. During her speech, I realized I wanted to inspire sales people!

It was not a coincidence that Don Hutson, an extremely successful speaker and sales trainer from my hometown, gave the keynote address at the convention. When I went home, my head was swimming with the possibilities. I began to understand how I could take the principles I believed and apply them to real life situations where people deal with issues in the business community.

At the suggestion of Sandy Karn, I called the president of the Positive Thinking Rallies. I met him, interviewed, and told him I could begin as soon as I put a load of clothes in the dryer. He asked, "Don't you want to go your Graduation?" I replied, "Oh yeah, that's right, my parents would probably appreciate that." I worked for the Positive Thinking Rallies and the American Sales Training Association for the next four years.

MENTORS

My career "on the road" began quickly. I was able to learn from some of the greatest teachers and trainers of our time. I listened to Zig Ziglar blend spiritual principles into ideas on sales and building your own business. I heard Cavett Robert talk about human engineering, motivation, and how to have integrity when dealing with people. The great Norman Vincent Peale spoke about disciplining your thought life, staying focused, and affirming the positive. He challenged people to cultivate and maintain the mental preparation needed for sustaining a faith oriented lifestyle. Dr. Robert Schuller's message on "Possibility Thinking" strengthened the framework by providing exploration for creative alternatives and solutions.

I loved having a chance to sit, listen, have meals with, and learn from these men and women. One day I had the privilege to pick up Earl Nightingale. I asked him, "If I was your son and I was starting my life and career, what would be important for me to know?"

He told me there were two truths he shared with his own son that pretty much summed it up. "First, you become what you think about all day long. And second, you reap exactly what you sow — and then some." At the time, I thought this was pretty simplistic and said, "OK, what else?"

He replied, "That's it."

The more I thought about it, the more I understood those two axioms for living. If we get clear on what we're thinking, affirming, and believing, we will realize how it shapes what we become. Likewise, the energy level invested in something will determine the results.

I can also vividly recall some special times when I had the opportunity to be the aid of Dr. Norman Vincent Peale. Dr. Peale was slight in stature, however, he was a powerful presenter. There was so much depth of character and personal conviction in his message and life that, when he took the stage, he seemed ten feet tall. At a press conference, my job was to oversee the proceedings and let the reporters know when Dr. Peale had answered enough questions. Then, Dr. Peale would wrap up and I'd usher him out of the room. I was always impressed that Dr. Peale always asked me to show him to a place where he could collect his thoughts and pray after the press conference in preparation for his presentation.

When I began we were sent in to a city and would be given a couple of hundred tickets to barter with. We were instructed to take a cab from the airport if we didn't drive, to one of the largest car dealers in town. Then we were to trade half of our "comp" tickets for the use of a car to use to make calls, a "loaner car". Then if the first dealer wouldn't do it we were to go to another and another until we found one who would trade or barter. Then with transportation we would begin to line up a place to stay. We would repeat this process with the larger hotels in town until we had a room for the next six weeks, or we could pay our own expenses. After we were set up then we had earned the right to make thirty cold calls a day in person for the next six weeks. After doing this for four years I remembered thinking to myself, "you know, if I can do this I can do just about anything".

Being on the road for six to eight weeks at a time, making thirty cold calls a day, was a tremendous learning experience. However being with great teachers and role models helped me prepare for fulfilling my direction.

William J. McGrane, Jr. was the most instrumental person in shaping my direction. Bill McGrane died in 1991, and his profound impact remains. In McGrane's quest to discover the answer to "Why do people hurt so much?", his work became researching self-esteem. He held intensive weekend seminars that were an experiential, discovery learning process.

Bill McGrane developed a "discovery learning" style by asking well-designed questions to let people come up with the answers for themselves. He realized that when others simply tell you things, you will discount the teaching unless you experience results for yourself. These experiences allowed you to get to the core of your pain in order to discover the underlying influences that impact your life and relationships.

His philosophy (and the philosophy of the McGrane Institute) emphasizes that most of our personal pain is a result of "value judging". We value judge ourselves first, then others to a similar level. We require or expect others to live their lives based on what we know and believe. McGrane believed that value judging was at the core of personal pain. He taught that the antidote to pain was total unconditional love and comprehensive acceptance. This he referred to as TUA—Total Unconditional Acceptance.

Value judging will many times reveal itself in our language. We imply shame, blame, guilt, and remorse with words like should, ought, and must.

My facade stemmed from trying to please everyone and always falling short of the mark. Bill McGrane became a mentor and directed me to discover something that was missing in my life. I chose to give up the tendency to compare myself with others. I focused on adjusting my language and thoughts to be in keeping with my new, more accurate understanding of myself.

These concepts allowed me to stop talking about it and start *living* what I believed in every area. I learned how to truly "listen" as well as how to ask questions—questions that would help me to help others work through personal issues. My goal is helping people in sales deal with personal issues and business barriers, things that are holding them back and preventing them from being as successful as they can be.

When I met Bill McGrane in 1978, he cared enough to confront me in a method he called "carefronting." He asked, "What do you want to do with your life?"

I answered, "I want to speak and teach."

Then he asked, "How come you don't speak? How come you're promoting other people and not sharing your own message?"

The reason was that I didn't think I had a message. I thought I was too young and needed to have more life experience and "hard knocks" in order to have any credibility. I responded by telling him that I didn't think I was ready yet. He told me to "Just begin where you are."

I told him the reason I wasn't ready was because I was comparing myself to all these great speakers like Paul Harvey, Art Linkletter, Norman Vincent Peale, Zig Ziglar, Cavett Robert, and every other luminary the rallies enlisted. I kept asking myself, "What do I have to say that is more important than these people with all of their experience and their preparation?" I wanted to find out how to develop my own story. I asked Bill McGrane, "How do I find what my topics are?"

He told me, "Begin where you are. What are the issues you've overcome and what are the lessons learned from those areas you've been wrestling with?"

All of my issues were centered around a lack of confidence in my abilities; I questioned my value and worth. I asked, "Am I able to accept myself unconditionally? If guilt, shame, and outside pressure weren't present, would I lose my will to work?" I wasn't sure what else would motivate me.

I was a talker, not a doer. He showed me how to take action. I needed to stop analyzing, thinking, and talking about what I wanted to do and actually begin to have an impact. I decided to start sharing what I had recently learned about dealing with and overcoming rejection in a selling environment.

Allowing ourselves to have what we need is a self-esteem issue. Bill McGrane also modeled how you can live with intact self-esteem, integrating it into your daily behavior. He once said, "Energy begets energy. So don't put energy into anything you don't want to get bigger." I began to realize that if I chose the direction I put my energy into, that area would come to life. I began to think I could take a different direction rather than trying to be just like my teachers. I began to see that I didn't have to use somebody else's material or somebody else's style. I could use my personal history to shape my message.

My early belief was that the "image" I wanted the world to see might be in jeopardy if I didn't fulfill external expectations. So I used a facade until I realized that my acceptance of myself didn't need to be based on how well I pleased others. I began to move from being outer driven to being more inner directed.

While I was wrestling with these types of questions, I started studying self-esteem ideas. This began a 20-year connection with the McGrane Institute. I wanted to learn how to impact people in a life changing manner. So I began working through some of the self-esteem and value judging issues. I had to first learn to separate myself from my performance. Often, I marveled at the skill with which McGrane would present his questions to gently, yet directly, help a person address their pain. He was a teacher who helped me understand the growing process.

At the same time, I was learning as much as I could from the rally circuit. After the program, I would zealously ask many questions in order to learn how to develop further. In my in depth learning experience with William J. McGrane, he identified a unique factor in my life story. He shared with me that that common thread throughout was that I always seemed to be helping or facilitating others in finding their direction. My unique factor and role are directing others. The last eighteen years I have researched this concept.

THE DIRECT METHOD OF LEARNING AND GROWTH

The "Direct Method" is my term for the process that allows us to grow and develop our skills.

D   determine your personal focus

I   integrate new information

R   responsible for resources

E   experience the experience

C   comparison to creativity

T   telling the truth

THE "D" OF DIRECT STANDS FOR "DETERMINE YOUR PERSONAL FOCUS"

First, envision your purpose. Ask yourself:

- What is really important to me?

- What is my purpose for developing my skills and abilities?

- What is my purpose for starting my own business and/or what do I want to do next?

Our purpose is the compelling reason for doing what we are now ready to do. It is sufficient for the motivation needed to follow through and complete the challenge. Dave McNally in his book *Even Eagles Need a Push* states, "The antithesis of having a purpose is the empty life where there is no meaning, where the daily objective is survival."

First, take a moment and think about your purpose. Listen to the purposes behind your commitments. Your purpose can "show up" in the reason you want to develop your skills and move upward in your career. Your purpose can indicate internal drives or reasons you accept additional responsibility. Clearly, truly successful people are contributors. They are in love with life and all the possibilities before them. Their accomplishments are rooted in a desire to grow and be of service to humanity.

Next, identify your core criteria. Core criteria is knowing what you need, want, and value most in your life and career. When you identify your core criteria, you have developed a yardstick by which to measure your satisfaction. Simply list what you need, want, and value most.

Then, focus on limitations awareness. Ask yourself, "What are my limitations or undeveloped areas at this stage in my life?"

Your limitations might include skills and characteristics that are necessary for producing the outcomes you want for the next phase of your life. If you know what skills are in place and what's missing, then you can assess what you need to develop to fulfill your chosen direction.

Ask yourself, "What are the skill areas that I need to develop in order to produce the outcome I want?" You could be dealing with time constraints or other conflicts. If you have something you need to remove, be aware of your limitations and begin to address them. This is the important phase that clears your pathway for growth.

The degree to which we are willing to remove any known barrier and make growth a high priority marks our level of commitment. Our confidence level helps determine our personal focus.

Many of us have the tendency to desire others' unique qualities. At the beginning of their career, people are trying to figure out their own unique factors. This growth process comes in stages. Level one is "unconscious, incompetent." Here you don't even know you don't know! In level two, you become a "conscious, incompetent." This is where you know you don't know and that you have work to do. (Isn't it comforting to know that realizing what you don't know is actually part of the growth process?) Now that you know what you're missing, you can begin to learn on purpose. Level three is called the "conscious, competent." You know what to do and do more of it. Level four is when you learn, layer after layer, gradually growing in competence until you naturally have become an "unconscious, competent."

Commit to the activities that remove your barriers. Some of these may take a little bit of time and effort, yet if you devote energy to growth you will see results. Bill McGrane said, "It takes fifteen years to become an overnight success. The first year we have some degree of clumsiness. The second year some degree of competence. Then the third year some degree of excellence."

He also states, "The person with the knowledge can gain the skill, and the person with the skill can change their circumstances. The choice is mine, escape into a mind-numbing activity or prepare for the future."

THE "I" STANDS FOR "INTEGRATE NEW INFORMATION"

How many of you, as you begin a new direction, also begin to integrate new information? Integrating new information is where most of us begin expanding our limited knowledge.

Inspirational teachers and role models can teach you things they have learned. However, we also risk comparing our skills with someone else's expertise. We say, "Wow, one of these days I'd like to grow up and be just like you. I want to learn to say everything like you and do everything like you. Not only that, I want to think that you do everything just the way I want to. How do you do that? How do you know that?"

However, we need to be careful not to compare ourselves by thinking, "I could never do that. I could never ask anybody to come to a function, or whatever we might say to ourselves." Comparison is when we judge ourselves harshly and believe we are inadequate to accomplish the task. We need to be careful to learn from others without internalizing feelings of inferiority, especially in the area of skill development.

In order to find mentors, we need to look to people we admire and respect with whom we would like to enter into a teaching/learning relationship. Linda Phillips Jones, in her book *Mentors and Protegees*, defines five stages of the integrated learning relationship.

Phase 1: Mutual Admiration

Phase one in the five phases of a mentor/protegee relationship is mutual admiration. Mutual admiration is like the honeymoon phase and the mentor says, "Wow, they're fantastic, I think they could be my protegee. I know they could excel; they are just that sharp." And you may say, "Wow, I want to be just like them when I grow up. They do things just as I hope to some day. I finally found somebody I can really believe in." And that's where it begins, the honeymoon phase.

Phase 2: Development

And then phase two, development. And guess who's doing most of the giving during the development phase? The mentor is, and who's doing most of the receiving? The student, and so this is when the teacher is sharing their wisdom and the student is learning, and then that gives way to stage three.

Phase 3: Disillusionment

Would you agree that if you're involved with anybody over a period of time, mistakes will be made and things will not necessarily turn out the way you expect? On either side. So then, level three is disillusionment. This is when the mentor says, "You didn't follow through. I'm disappointed in you. I thought you were committed to learning and growing." And the student says, "Well, what's the use, because you forgot to give me the information you promised, I've been waiting on you."

And so, reality is that there are some slight disappointments on both sides, and so what ends up happening is that the disillusionment sets in and the teacher says, "Well, they're not following through on their commitments, they say they're ready, but they're not taking action. I don't know whether to believe what they say or what they're doing." And that's only fair. And the student says, "Well, I thought that they were everything and I didn't think they were going to make these mistakes. Now I realize that they are human and that I need to adjust my expectations; I don't know if this is what I thought it was going to be, and I don't know if I want to do more yet."

Phase 4: Parting.

And then phase four. Let's say that the student or protegee continues to grow and develop; there could be a time when parting would take place or begin to take place. And it's a healthy phase in the process. The fact of the matter is that, as the student begins to accept responsibility for themselves, and who they are, they will initiate the parting phase themselves. And you will want your mentor to delegate more things to you, let you participate more; then you will begin to pull away from a dependence on your mentor. This scenario is the healthier way to grow and move on.

Another way would be to stay a little too long at a level of development less than you are able but more than you are willing to accept responsibility for actually doing. This situation breeds resentment on the part of the student or protegee toward the mentor. The student becomes envious of the position and power the mentor holds. This can lead to the student becoming disloyal and undermining the teacher or mentor.

Phase 5: Transformation.

Then stage five is transformation. I believe this is when you make the transformation into the mentor role yourself. And you say to your mentor, who at one time you just admired from a distance, "You know, at one time you were the teacher but now I can teach too and you will always be my mentor. However, I want you to know that I feel like I've earned the respect of my peers and that I have a lot that I can offer also." And a transformation has taken place. And you, as a mentor and as a protegee also are saying that you have gone through this process and now you are ready to help other people go through it and emerge into a higher level of growth and responsibility.

THE "R" STANDS FOR BECOMING "RESPONSIBLE FOR RESOURCES"

Number one: "Read the Need." After you begin to move from the relationship with your mentor, look for ways to use your own ideas. Begin to share from your own experiences. Don't wait to be told what to do any more. Trust your own ability to determine what needs to be done.

Number two: "Initiate individuality." You are becoming an individual, using the knowledge gained from your learning experiences. You learn from the classes you attend, the books you read, and the people you associate with, but most importantly, you learn from personal experience. Begin to share your own creative insights; learn to trust you have ideas that work.

Number three: "Accept responsibility for your unique factors." Develop YOUR unique factors. Don't compare yourself with others by wishing you had their abilities instead of your own. This book and the Direct method are an example of how I have done this. Bill McGrane gave me the word Direct as a unique factor in 1980. I've developed it into a one hour talk, a one day seminar and now a book.

Number four: "Your self-esteem awareness increases at this point." You now know you can make a valid contribution.

Number five: "Begin to allow for personal discoveries." Personal discoveries, self-esteem, and unique factors become obvious when you diligently apply yourself. Personal discoveries come from heightened awareness and sustained involvement. Once you transition out of the "R" stage, you move from being directed by outside sources to a more responsible inner direction.

THE E STANDS FOR "EXPERIENCE THE EXPERIENCE"

Number one: "Live with feedback messages from your customers, clients and colleagues." They will let you know how well you're doing by the way they share their appreciation. Maintain your standard of satisfaction by listening to their feedback.

Number two: "Observe, perceive, and discover as you are experiencing the experience; learn the lessons that come out of that experience." Simply observe what you're doing a lot of. For example, what lessons can you learn from an especially busy or productive week?

Repetition is just practice. The more you practice, the more confident you become. Could you share encouragement with someone else, based on your experience? Of course you could!

Number three: "Identify the processes of the lessons you are learning." I am constantly clarifying how to find my direction. Often, describing the process behind the lessons you have learned is extremely helpful.

Number four: "Test your discoveries and confirm your observations." Do your own homework and research projects. Identify what works and what does not work for you as you are increasing your experience in business.

Number five: "Refine your skills through experience." If you attempt to refine your skills by mentally rehearsing, analyzing your thoughts or self criticism, you will not move forward. Take action and give yourself more room to make mistakes. You will increase your activity and refine outcomes.

I worked with a client who paid his Senior Vice-President $700 for making a mistake that cost the company $7,000. He told me the reason was because he wanted executives to learn how to be more creative and not be so fearful of making mistakes. He also wanted them to accept responsibility for that level of leadership. So, he rewarded the behavior he wanted from the executives.

THE "C" STANDS FOR MOVING FROM "COMPARISON TO CREATIVITY"

Victor Frankl relates what he learned from his experience as a prisoner in Auschwitz. He writes about how everything can be taken from a person except—the last of the human freedoms—the ability to choose one's attitude in any given set of circumstances, to choose one's own way.

Number one: "Begin preparing your own message." Do you already have a message about your experiences ready to share with others? Most people have a message about life lessons that they can share through stories and in support of others. You've already experienced both of these things. Your business or personal growth will allow you to appreciate things you have already learned and apply them in such a way that people can benefit from you. I believe you feel really great when you can help someone by sharing something you have already been through.

Number two: "Trust your own inner knowing process." This intuition doesn't necessarily have to be validated from other people. Trust yourself or spend quiet time in prayerful reflection, trusting the still small voice inside.

This comes from experience, observing, learning from, and trusting the ideas that come to you. You can learn from an existing system that requires personal comparisons. Then move into your own experience. Ask yourself, "I want to do my best. . . What would be a way I could refine my process to produce the outcomes I'm after? What do I just 'know' I need to say or do next?" Continue to refine and polish your outcomes as you learn to trust your intuition. Through this process, your personal signature will begin to emerge.

Number three: "Identify who benefits." It could be your team or a group of people who you want to train. Select the components of your presentation so that the message will be appropriate to help the people who will benefit to reach their desired outcome.

Number four: "Share as you prepare." There comes the time in virtually every interaction when we instinctively know a lesson we have previously learned could benefit another. If we then open up and become a coach or mentor, sharing unselfishly from our experience, it might facilitate a breakthrough for them. This kind of timely self disclosure can have an immense impact on others.

Number five: "Self disclosure begins." After you have experience, guess what?. . . you have more to say. I overheard a couple of mid-level management people in a direct sales company say they we're going to go through qualification for upper level management again. I asked, "How come?" And they replied, "We've been listening to the top National Sales Directors in our company and we know that when they reach the National level that they give those speeches and they always have these great stories to tell and we figured that if we went through our qualification twice, then that would make our stories better." I said, "Hey, that's one alternative, and you can do that. However, do you believe it's possible that by the time you become a National level executive you will have mastered challenges much greater than that of going through qualification twice? Believe me. . . It will be more than enough. You might not need to do that." They acknowledged, "Well, we never thought about that." So I said, "Well, you think about that."

Let me share how self disclosure began for me when I was getting started. Remember. . . when you began your career, you memorized everybody else's material, learned their buzz words and their powerful scripting techniques. That's what I did. When I was working with Zig Ziglar, Cavett Robert, and Don Hutson, I knew all of their best material. (I still know a lot of their best material.)

Each time we have an election year, I am reminded of one of Cavett Robert's favorite stories. The Whiskey Story was and is one of Cavett's trademarks. Consequently, he used it at virtually every seminar. We all looked forward to the time when he would tell the "Great Whiskey Story". We would practice his stories in the elevators, trying to do our best Cavett Robert imitation and then listen with rapt attention to his speeches.

THE WHISKEY STORY

Cavett Robert would say. . . "Down in my native state of Mississippi, down where prohibition still has its strongest citadel, a little paper called the Macon Beacon in Noxabe county had the unadulterated gall, mind you, to ask a local politician where he stood on the whiskey question.

"Now in Noxabe county during the prohibition, if you were *for* whiskey, you would get half the vote and lose half. But if you were *against* whiskey, you'd get half the vote and lose half the vote. You were damned if you did and damned if you didn't.

"But I thought this local politician acquitted himself quite well when he said, "Sir, if, when you say whiskey, you mean that poison scourge that topples the righteous man and woman from the pinnacles of gracious living down to the bottomless pit of despair, verily I say, takes the very bread out of the mouth of Babes, then I want you to write in your paper that I will fight against this demon with all the strength that I possess.

"BUT if, when you say whiskey, you mean that oil of conversation that puts a spring in the old man's step on a frosty morn, puts untold millions in our treasury, builds schools, playgrounds, makes this world a better place in which to live, I want you to write in your paper that I will fight for this essence of Divinity with all the strength that I possess."

Then he put the crowning glory, the capstone of it all, on top when he said, "Sir, I am a man of my conviction, I will not compromise, this is my stand!"

FINDING MY OWN STORY

I listened to Cavett, thinking, "I hope one day I can have my own trademark story and everyone will know it is my story when I tell it." For the longest time, I didn't have my own story; I told Robert's story, I told Ziglar's story, I told McGrane's story, or Nightingale's story. *I told everybody else's stories!*

I would memorize these stories saying to myself, 'You know, I feel like I'm getting there, and at the same time, there's more that I need to be doing." There was a time in 1984, after I had been speaking for five or six years, that I had one of the most difficult times in my career. I thought I was going to absolutely go out of business.

My business (along with the whole industry) was in a downturn and I had to make a decision whether I would survive it. One day I got an idea while I was shaving. So I sat down on the floor in the bathroom and started writing down my idea. I finally went into the office with shaving cream still on my face and wrote about four or five pages. It just tumbled out and became my signature poem. As I wrote I realized I was ready to get back to work. Quitting was not an option.

Writing this poem helped me develop my story as well as understand that even when things weren't working, I didn't have to compromise my commitment. My commitment was not based on what was happening on the outside; instead, I needed to focus on what was taking place on the inside.

ON THE ROAD AGAIN

I was sitting in church wondering what he said,
to cause what was happening in my head,
to cause me to feel deep in the pit of me
that because of how those words were spoken
my hurtful and damaging behavior was broken.

I didn't know what he had done,
but I began to feel that I was one
who had born in him a great desire
to know just how a life to inspire.

So I sold many seminars and rallies then
to learn what I could from great women and men.
I paid my dues, like I'd been told,
everything of value had to be sold.
I learned my craft and developed my skills
and found this way of life a test of will.

I joined the National Speakers Association in 1977
and thought I'd stepped on into Heaven.
To view people God used to leaven a world scorned with
sorrow and consternation
with uplifting voices and information.

Some were serious, some funny, some real smart,
but they all sent messages to my heart.

Sandy Karn, Dr. Tonning, and Don Hutson to begin,
then Cavett and Zig put their wisdom in.
Why those big oaks took time with this little twig
I did not know
it wasn't until later that it began to show.
I will be like them, I would say to myself,
I would memorize things from my books on the shelf.
I would wear their clothes, I would dream their dreams,
and my mind was transformed out of its seams.
I asked myself how can I get better,
and I had no idea what I would learn later.

The McGrane family continued the growing trend
developing what I had learned to a greater end.
With self-esteem and pointed sweat questions
and concepts that took much mental digestion.
They said, take more books down off the shelf
but begin sharing the message within yourself,
you're the one with the story to tell
and if you share that message well,
you help free people from their own personal hell.

So I stopped trying to decide who I'd like to be
and finally decided just to be me,
the person that God wants you to see.
So, I had my message and I'd lived it through
and now it was flavored with a person who
had the knowledge, skill and power
to share a life changing discourse in a day or an hour.
I've spoken too much and I've spoken too little
now I'm looking for a schedule that's in the middle.
Even though I have this life history,
there are still some questions that become a mystery,
that some tempting and destructive force sends
when we have no strength to deny or defend.

We ask ourselves when we get through speaking or teaching
did the people really get what they were seeking?
Did it really make a difference after all?
Was my impact large or was it small?
Does it really make a difference in the scheme of things
or just the tinkling brass of the cymbal that rings?

Then out of the crowd comes a person so dear,
they wait a little longer in the rear,
you know they're touched, you see the tear,
and they say 'I almost didn't come tonight,
my spouse and I, we just had a fight.
But now I know the reason I came,
your message was more than more of the same,
you knew my needs, you guided my path,
how in a million years could I express
the difference you made with this address.'

Then I'd share you need not say,
It is I who doesn't know just how to thank
a person who would pause before they left
and give me such a precious gift.
The truth is I paused tonight before my talk,
and asked if this is the way God wanted me to walk.
Your response tells me this is more than just work,
it's a light to shine where it is dark,
a smile to stretch into a grin
and a heartstring to pluck and pull within.

So I know it's late and I need to go
and rest my head for my next show...
to rise and catch a flight and then
finally get back on the road again...

Bill Cantrell

I want you to know that when I wrote that out, I knew that I was where I needed to be. And I know that your response might be that it's more powerful for me to share my own message than it is for me to share something I've memorized from somebody else. And it is the same way with you and the people you influence. They will trust you, when they know that you're sharing an authentic experience from your heart. It was at this point in my life that I knew I was more internally directed. External challenges are things we can overcome. I call this transition moving from. . . Prose to Poetry. By the way, I've been writing poetry to capture my life lessons ever since.

THE "T" STANDS FOR SIMPLY "TELLING THE TRUTH"

Number one: "Identify the information that you have acquired," give credit to the people you have learned from. For example, I have given credit to teachers like Cavett Robert, Don Hutson, Dr. Waylon Tonning, Sandy Karn, Zig Ziglar, Bill McGrane, Ms. Aste, and my parents. I feel a sense of responsibility to those who have contributed to helping me find my direction. I hope I will do something worthwhile with the teachings they have taken care to give me.

Number two: "Identify the discovered insights from the things you've learned from others and also your original material." There are going to be certain messages that are your own. My messages are keeping my self-esteem intact, overcoming obstacles, and maintaining successful behaviors in the midst of adversity, made possible because I learned lessons from my experiences. Making 30 cold calls a day, moving through depression, and preventing rejection from stopping my work helped me customize my communication skills.

Leadership, to me, is being willing to say "yes" every time someone invited me to do something that stretched me, scared me half to death, yet at the same time caused me to grow. My Pastor invited me to fill in at the pulpit once when he went on vacation. I had never preached in front of my church congregation. I bought five books and studied for a month. I had enough material for a five day conference. I only needed to speak for 20 minutes. So, the day before, I threw away all my notes. My sermon then consisted of sharing a meaningful lesson from personal experience. Because I said "yes" there, I could also say "yes" to other opportunities. What are your messages that are waiting to be heard?

Number three: "Know the outcome that you want as you share your experiences with the people that you are leading." I know the outcome I want for you as you read this book. I want you to accept responsibility for doing what you need to do now, so the future you dream about can become a reality. Also I hope this book allows you to focus and feel confident as your skills and character are developing, so that you're ready to move into leadership positions more readily than before. Progress is an ongoing process of accepting responsibility for your own learning and growth.

Number four: "Process your results." Did you get the outcome you were going for? If not, what did you learn, how can you refine your process, help your clients, and experience the experience you want for them and for yourself.

Number five: "Live congruently." Actually do what you say you believe. Peter Lord stated, "What you do is what you believe, everything else is just words." That is one of my favorite quotes because I believe people are always watching us to see if they can trust us.

Live what you believe so that people are able to learn lessons from watching you as much as from listening to you. Live your message.

People who live honestly, take responsibility, and tell the truth will not be unduly influenced by their environment. They will not always be seeking approval from others or rearranging their approach to protect themselves. Instead, they will give of themselves through service, find their messages as they gain experience, and simply tell the truth to people who desire to learn.

PREPARING FOR LEADERSHIP

For the longest time, I believed that my mistakes and undeveloped areas disqualified me from high levels of leadership or accomplishment. These things did matter, however not the way I originally believed. Instead, life events helped me to become who I always had dreamed of being—me.

When I asked, "What has been your greatest challenge, in your life so far, that you have overcome? What personal lesson did this challenging life event teach you?", a woman in the Midwest shared how her daughter had threatened to drop out of school at the age of fourteen. This was the same age the mother had been when she gave birth to the daughter. The mother had decided to go back to school and acquire her GED certificate. She didn't stop there, she went on to graduate from college, and ultimately had earned a master's degree. Because of the mother's example, the daughter decided to stay in school.

The mother's success story doesn't end there. She decided after completing her education to take on a challenge and start a business out of her home with a direct sales organization. She reasoned, "If I can get my master's degree at 38 years of age, I can do just about anything."

Another person in the Houston area had been a competitive gymnast until a horrendous automobile accident crushed her leg. Her dreams of competing internationally were dashed. She resolved to rehabilitate her crushed leg so she could compete in one last meet before retiring. It took four and a half years. She didn't place or win a ribbon, however she did win a great victory over her circumstances. She told me she learned a lot about herself as she confronted that challenge. She discovered the lessons that our greatest disappointments and challenges, as well as our most satisfying accomplishments, teach us how they prepare us for leadership.

A woman in Fayetteville, Arkansas, told me she was on food stamps and had been living in a shelter. Within a few years she found work, went back to school at night, and eventually purchased her own house. She was able to do this as an abandoned single woman with three children.

Sometimes I wonder how people make it through these hardships. It seems a strong faith in God, a loving family, and encouraging friends are extremely important during the difficult times. As you review your life history, mark the major events in your life. Who were your teachers throughout life? How could you take what you learn from your life events and begin sharing your lessons with others now?

LIFE'S LESSONS

We are conceived neither boy or girl,

Simply a person with our needs a whirl.

This is how we all begin,

All of heaven's potential packed within.

From our safe haven of mother's arm,

We all are shielded from serious harm.

We find ourselves journey bound.

Our universe feeds us from all around.

We venture out from the safe cocoon,

As if a visitor who had arrived too soon.

We are fed, clothed, and taught the truth,

According to our family roots.

If it's from our family, it has to be fact—

These teachers of ours surely do not lack.

We grow with pain or safe but strong,

Our family universe can't be wrong.

We learn, in the next stage of our trip,

Through education and religious scholarship.

With the rights and wrongs, goods and bads,

We fashion a map with the training we've had.

We break away knowing it all—

What's that that goes before a fall?

Our choices made, we are sure,

That we'll reach our destination, no detour.

The trip continues with one unwise turn,

We really believe that we have learned.

We vow to keep to the straight and narrow,

but the path is littered with doubt and sorrow.

How could life really be this way

living in denial is how we spend our days.

By changing our views based on the lessons we learned

We try again after we've been burned.

From high hopes, to near death we continue on

our arrogance and pride are almost gone.

Through adversity our creed is hammered out

We're tougher, smarter and stronger, no doubt.

So character may not be something society can teach

Only a maturity that living life helps us reach.

We now know what we believe from our own life's story

Making a difference then becomes our only hope for glory.

Bill Cantrell

FOOD FOR THOUGHT

- Who are the teachers and mentors who made a major difference in your life?

- Do you currently have someone who is shaping your direction and influencing your learning? Who? How?

- Are you on a lifelong learning program, consciously choosing the next phase of your preparation? What is the next phase for you?

- Do you believe that this kind of focused learning program, from a role model for you, is necessary to fully utilize your gifts and develop your own direction. If so, how?

CHAPTER 4

Branches

When I was ready to graduate from college, I sat down with my father and talked with him about my future. I needed to let him know I wanted to go my own way, try my own wings. It was exciting to think about the possibilities. Still, it meant we wouldn't be working together. I would miss that connection with my baseball coach, sales trainer, role model for business, and of course, Dad. The branch on a tree is part of the tree, yet it grows away from the tree. When we branch out on our own, or take a different turn in our direction, we begin to assess our preparation. That's the reason it's so important to have our skills in place and an experience base. We need to remind ourselves that we're ready to take on a new challenge and more growth. I believe that one of the things that postpones or prevents us from taking the challenge to branch out are deep feelings that influence us. Our identity, even our self-esteem, is going to be affected by being involved in selling. When we put ourselves on the line, we may become fearful because risk taking causes us to question ourselves all the way to the core.

If our self-esteem is intact, and we're emotionally healthy, there is no way that what people say or do can affect us. When we are internally prepared, we can keep our commitment to ourselves to branch off and move on. This branching process entails preparing our heart and mind to do what we now know is our direction for life.

Finding our direction, whatever our chosen profession may be, is accepting responsibility for contending with whatever life has brought our way and addressing those issues with integrity. We take our gifts, talents and abilities and use them in a way that doesn't deny ourselves what we need, what we want, or what's important for serving other people.

The process of finding our direction is like a flowing river, constantly moving and changing with the seasons. It evolves and grows and is dynamic. For example, if you make a choice of a career but it only contributes to your financial security, then that's not a healthy choice for your overall direction. You can choose to work primarily for money, but it doesn't mean it's going to satisfy some of the other needs you may have. Whether you want to include other areas or not, they are affected by your choice of where you go with your life and the reason you do the things that you do.

Some people will work only for the money and then spend all of their free time in serving, learning, and growing. In essence, they are attempting to make up for the loss of work satisfaction with their personal life. I prefer to blend things together by having my profession be closely involved in my learning, growth, and satisfaction. That's how, as a professional, I show people how they can accomplish what they want from their business and life. Once they set their course and they make a decision, like "I'm going to start this business on my own", they may have issues with which to contend. They can take the issues into consideration or not, the different choices produce very different outcomes. If they choose to deal with their issues, I believe there will be personal pay offs that will allow them to be more congruent, honest, true to themselves, and help them achieve personal integrity. They could even take a new direction altogether.

Living and working with internal integrity means living according to what you believe and what you've learned about yourself. For instance, I was talking with a woman who was discussing her husband's heart disease and how he wouldn't follow the doctors orders about his diet. That goes back to how we accept responsibility for hereditary influences, alcoholism, co-dependency, heart disease, cancer, or whatever. If you have a tendency towards dysfunctional behaviors that are an effect of a dysfunctional early childhood, you have a choice: whether to continue those behaviors or patterns, or to stop them.

Of course, our children will have issues with which to contend when they grow up. There are ways we can help our children learn to handle their lives in such a way to give them the best chance of being healthy.

What if our roots determined what worked best for us in our early pattern development, based on what we needed then? What if we are still fulfilling what those patterns encouraged us to do then? Are we on automatic pilot? Are we just robots, so once these patterns are set we are somehow required to carry them out? Can we make conscious decisions about how to refine our choices? Someone once said, "The sad truth of the matter is that most of us die with our music still in us." If we don't choose our best direction, we settle for less.

Larry Wilson tells a story about the time when his son was the quarterback for a Big 10 football team. He said that his son broke his leg and started ballet as a form of physical therapy. To his father's chagrin, his son discovered he liked ballet and eventually became a ballet artist. The dad had a difficult time accepting this as he'd always seen his son as "the quarterback, a chip off the old block." Now, his son was a "ballerina" and that was really tough for his father.

When he finally went to see him perform, Larry had a major insight about his life. In the musical "Fiddler on the Roof," Tevye, the father, sings a song called, 'Life is Like a Fiddler'. While Tevye tries to play his tune and eke out his song, he also has to keep from falling off the roof! Larry realized that, for himself and most of the people he'd worked with, this was how they lived their life—hanging on for dear life to the roof, desperately trying not to fall off, trying to get an elbow up so they can play their tune on their violin. Then they hold onto the roof for dear life, afraid that if they let go they'll lose what they have.

What if there is more to life, however you won't let it in out of fear? Can you settle for less and justify it somehow in your own mind?

SETTLING FOR MORE

Many of us have parents who were impacted by the Depression and by World War II, when rationing was commonplace and people didn't have enough to go around. Baby boomers are living in a time of affluence. Still, many of us still have a difficult time "receiving." According to Paul Harvey, we live in the world's richest nation. Although we only have six percent of the earth's surface and seven percent of the earth's population, we own and enjoy over fifty-four percent of the wealth in the world. We live in a land of opportunity and yet we continue to hold ourselves back. We often settle for only meeting our basic needs when there's so much more available. If we actually live the life we believe, we can have the courage of our convictions to take a stand, make a mark, and do those things we value in life.

Business philosopher Jim Rohn was once talking with a group of psychiatrists and he said to them, "Would you like to know what I think most affects the human mind?"

They said yes—they were very interested. Mr. Rohn said, "What I believe most affects the human mind is simply doing less than you're able, and *knowing* you're doing less than you're able when you do it."

There's something that bothers us when we settle for less than we know we're able to produce. For many of us, there are times in our lives when we've made a conscious choice to live beneath our own personal standards. We don't get what we need or want, we settle for less, and we know we're not living a life that lines up with what we deem important.

If we say we believe things but no one sees that in our actions, what does that say? If we don't make the conscious choice to live according to what's most important to us, how does that affect us? My personal experience is that this opens the door for self-condemnation to come in, for regrets, and for questions about our own personal integrity. It says much that we're not willing to do what it would take for us to live what we believe. Instead, we live a life that is characterized by hanging onto the edge of the roof for dear life.

Many people dream, however that doesn't mean they're living their dreams out in their life. If there is no action, the dream is only a fantasy or a mental apparition. If we focus, can we actually make our dreams come true? We need to ask ourselves, "What would need to exist for us to begin to make these things happen?"

LEARNING TO LIVE WHAT WE BELIEVE

If I say I believe it's important to "Love thy neighbor as thyself", then I need to ask myself first of all 'Do I love myself?' If I can't love myself, that obviously has an impact on whether I can love my neighbor. And what if I do love my neighbor as myself—yet I don't care much for myself? Can that be the reason I'm not able to love my neighbor very well? There may be issues that are preventing me from accepting myself totally and unconditionally.

One of the ways I gradually began to clarify this for myself was with a model that helped me understand the components of self-esteem— which included learning about self-respect. Although I understood what unconditional acceptance of myself and others meant, my image and self-worth were based more on external performance. It was based on the clothes I wore, the car I drove, the house I lived in, my zip code, and a lot of other things.

MODEL FOR SELF-ESTEEM

Here is a model to use to see where self-esteem comes from. This model, that describes the components of self-esteem, was done by Dan Kaufman (based on the work of Michael O'Connor, the author of *People Smart.*) In this model, self-worth is (at the most) ten percent of where I get my self-respect and self-esteem. It's based on needs. Maslow, in his hierarchy of needs, talked about different levels:

Survival: which would include air, water, food, rest, shelter, and pleasure

Security: to know that one's survival or well-being is not in jeopardy, especially physical, emotional and financial.

Belonging: to be accepted by others, to be a part of one's social or work environment

Love: to be recognized as significant, to have a high sense of self-respect, to sense one's self and contributions in life as significant

Self-esteem: to sense one's self and one's contributions in life as significant, according to one's own evaluation

Self-actualizing: to grow and expand one's personal horizons, taking our God-given talents, gifts and abilities and utilizing them fully. Living the life we know we're capable of living without leaving any of our gifts, talents, and abilities under-utilized; to become all that we can become with what we've been given and with our personal history.

THE BASIS OF SELF-ESTEEM

If 10% or less of our self-esteem comes from self-worth, most of our self-worth comes from meeting our needs. Needs, as you know from Maslow's hierarchy, are gradually satisfied. That means that each need level has to be met before the next one can be approached. So, what we do and how we do it is the focus.

In sales, this is going to be where the comparison comes from. We may ask, "Did I say that properly? What if I had done things differently? This is too important for me to mess up, because if I don't make money, I can't meet my needs. I can't keep going." The pressure begins to build since we need to get our needs met. We try to get our self-esteem met from success experiences and the approval of others.

However, if we're trying to get our self-esteem from the approval of others and our success experiences, we create a pretty threatening environment for ourselves. We create a situation of comparison and competition, which lowers our self-esteem, leaving us wide open to feel hurt if we experience rejection.

First, you get some of what you need in life, then you want more. After getting more, then you want better. And when you get better, then you want different. Then it starts all over again—it's a never ending cycle. When we get caught up in that cycle, we never feel completely satisfied. Temporary satisfaction is the best that we can hope for. And when our sales are our primary way to meet our needs and to make money just to pay bills, we're going to be tempted to have our direction guided by this need for approval and never ending series of success accomplishments.

SELF-RESPECT

What if ninety percent, or virtually all of our self-esteem, comes from *self-respect*. Self-respect stems from our cognitive beliefs and our values. This is what drives our behavior to choose certain actions. To have self-respect, it's imperative that we live in alignment with our values. Acting in accordance to values, beliefs, and living by our standards is necessary if we wish to maintain personal integrity.

One of the main traps sales people fall into is a willingness to lower their standards, until they're no longer satisfied with themselves. When sales people don't live in accordance to their own values and standards, their ability to project confidence into the marketplace is diminished. When you are selling simply to meet a need, you become more at risk when rejection begins to come your way.

On the other hand, if you have a philosophy of life and a principled code you live by, your choices will reflect your standards. Consequently, you can build your business in a way that is most fulfilling for the long run. When you choose to honor your standards and operate from your values and beliefs, you keep your commitment to yourself first. This frees us to meet our needs without internal conflict shutting us down.

When we are in the process of branching out, "battling it out with our own conscience" is where much of our best energy and creativity goes rather than in pursuing our direction. Personally, I can motivate myself longer and deeper for my values than I can for getting my needs met temporarily.

SELLING BASED ON VALUES

Lawrence Kohlberg, Ph.D. wrote two books on moral development. In his volume, *The Philosophy Of Moral Development*, he outlines six distinct stages of development. Don Cipriano, a leader in education and training, has condensed Kohlberg's stages of moral development.

Stage One: Punishment-Obedience: Emphasis is on "Will I get into trouble for this?"

Stage Two: Instrumental Relativist: "What's in it for me? Will this make my life work better?"

Stage Three: Nice Person: "Is it nice to do that? What will others think of me?"

Stage Four: Law and Order: "Is it against the rules?"

Stage Five: Social Contract: "Did we agree to this?"

Stage Six: Universal Ethics: "What will happen to mankind and society in a world where people treat each other with respect?"

In the higher stages of development, we can place a greater emphasis on personal integrity. We can keep our standards high by choosing to set boundaries, determining what is acceptable and unacceptable. This is very encouraging. Whatever we sell, it will be more fulfilling, because it will be congruent and in alignment with who we are. We don't lower our standards. We live according to them.

When we do less than we are able and we know we're operating at a level below our standards, we are unforgiving of ourselves. I suggest that, instead of lowering our standards, we raise them up so that they're in keeping with the values and beliefs we hold. When you have boundaries, you know what's negotiable and what's non-negotiable. You have a benchmark to help you determine what business fits within those boundaries. You don't have to rely on feelings.

By far, the best way to handle rejection comes in knowing the difference between self-esteem and self-image.

ELIMINATING SHOULD, OUGHT, MUST FROM OUR THINKING

Our image is something we project based on what we feel we want to do or be. It's like the old adage of "Trying to keep up with the Jones'." We may try to look as if we're more successful than we are. So we spend a lot of money in hopes that we'll make more money. ("You need to spend money to make money"—however spend within reason!) Who are we really trying to impress? Impressing others has no future, it leads to value judging (yourself and others) and comparing.

One situation where we are often at risk is when we attend "conferences" with our colleagues and peers. If we are there to see how well we're doing, we could be in for a very painful experience. Again, if you go to get ideas, knowing your own standards beforehand, then it doesn't matter how well anybody else is doing. Having a "present" orientation allows us to decide what we want and need. Then we can get our missing pieces whenever we choose. This allows us to have a more present orientation when we come from a clear personal identity. If we choose to identify what we need, want and value, *we can accept ourselves more unconditionally and we will have a sense of self-respect, regardless of where we are in our business.*

For example, when our business is up, we respect who we are and when our business is off, our respect for ourselves is not affected. Simply because we have no need to compare. Business downturn, off times, and circumstances outside our control are going to happen. When we have an attitude of self-respect, environmental factors don't have the same influence on us. Our self-respect isn't in jeopardy of being compromised.

A dangerous myth today is that if we just set "goals and objectives", everything will be fine. So we try to meet certain goals and objectives that we either make or miss. Unfortunately, when we make them, we often feel as if we need to do more. And if we miss them, we feel like we're a failure. When we finally reach the objective, or get the outcome we're going for, what do we normally do? Many of us dance around, celebrate, take a month off, or feel no matter what we do it's never "enough."

YOU CAN'T GET THERE FROM HERE

If we operate out of "self-image" (trying to live up to "shoulds, oughts and musts" from our environment), then we are outer-driven. When we're outer-driven, no matter what we do, we're always way behind. We can never meet all the expectations people have for us. Expectations to live our faith, to contribute to the family income, to always meet the needs of our families first and then our career, are expectations that just can't all be met at once.

If we're not careful, our internal dialogue might sound like this: "Based on how old I am and how much money I've invested in my career, I'm supposed to be making a lot more money by now. My colleagues are doing great and have moved on without me."

You can see the potential for comparison that could begin to set in and kill our willingness to branch out and grow.

So, what often happens is we say to ourselves, "Well, if I could just get where I want to be. . ." We set up an imaginary or self-imposed benchmark. Then, every step along the way, we feel like we haven't made it yet and we're not okay. The worst part is that even if we make it — it's not going to be truly satisfying!

Here's the challenge: while we've been spending all our energy "making it", the "it" has moved. Because once you make it, new expectations get added to the list. And now, you don't have to just get there, you need to get way out there to make it. The finish line keeps moving further away! You feel as if no matter what you do, you can never be finished. You can't get there from here.

I believe this demoralizing, frustrating feeling prevents us from taking chances (like making calls and contacts) and putting ourselves out there. We avoid the feeling and the hurt by taking a mini-vacation ("You know today would be an excellent day to re-paper those shelves or sweep out the carport."). We find non-rejection activities to occupy our time. Or, we throw our hands up and say, "This isn't working so I'll just take today off and feel taken advantage of." We let ourselves feel victimized. That's when you know rejection's gotten you!

Whether or not you're doing well, whether or not you're making the money you need and meeting all those other needs you have really isn't the issue. It's doing less than you are able and not meeting your standards. The encouraging news is there's hope! When we learn to sustain our commitment to our direction, we can develop and refine the skills we need in order to move from just being survivors to being satisfied and prosperous.

The way to make this happen is instead of being outer-driven, being *inner-directed*. If we accept ourselves unconditionally, the way we are *now*, then it's possible to be inner-directed.

Some people don't know how to accept themselves unconditionally. The ultimate way to think about unconditional acceptance is to ask yourself if there's a Supreme Being. If you believe there is a God, do you believe God makes mistakes? Most people who believe in God think He doesn't make mistakes. If God doesn't make mistakes, then you are here for a reason. When we study the old and new testaments of the Bible, it gives us a true understanding of God's loving nature. In understanding God's love for us, we are free to accept ourselves unconditionally as well, without the "shoulds, oughts, and musts." A personal relationship with our Creator provides a firm foundation for our personal identity.

Then, in challenging times, when we doubt our purpose or place in the scheme of things, we know we are here for a very definite reason. Instead of being driven by what we *have* to do, we are directed based on our needs, wants, and our beliefs and values. We can be more inner-directed, because every step along the way, we know we're meeting our own internal standards rooted in beliefs and values.

Bear in mind, this is a process. The higher our unrealistic expectations, the greater our disappointment and disillusionment when things don't turn out the way we planned. If we haven't "made it", it's okay, because we're moving along the way. The idea is not to just reach an objective or one goal. *It's to have a lifestyle that works. . . to have a career that's satisfying, and a sense of fulfillment, knowing that what we are doing is important to us and that it lines up with who we are.*

Finding Your Direction is my descriptive phrase for the process of discovering what we are here to do—or not just barely make it, how we can prosper and live more abundantly. When I started out making those 30 cold calls a day, the reason it was so painful is that I was working to meet my needs for success and approval of others. When I understood the role self-esteem issues played, I realized *it's my responsibility to provide the reinforcement and the layering to protect myself* mentally and emotionally, so if I get a no, I know how to "position it" or handle it. I still work on it—sometimes daily! Yet I've found that selling or choosing to start a new venture or project is so much easier now!

What if you're in desperate straits? You can't make the mortgage or pay the bills. Of course, your focus will be on meeting essential needs to survive! However, that doesn't mean you're stuck! There are things you can begin to do now to branch out. It might mean acquiring additional training, or it might mean more marketing or selling. It may even mean becoming more efficient so you have time to pursue other options. So do first things first! Then make sure you begin to move towards the bigger picture. This is not a quick fix, short term approach. It will lead to an outcome that is ultimately more satisfying.

When I set up mutually beneficial agreements to meet the needs, wants, and values for both my client and myself, I no longer feel the need to martyr myself unnecessarily, just for that business. This gives me an outcome I can live with long term. Now, I don't have to fear that if I did get business, it would throw my life into turmoil. I don't have to be afraid of success.

How do we keep the momentum to "keep on keeping on?" The next step is to find something to sufficiently motivate us. Going from excitement for one product to another provides a little extra boost, yet not the foundational motivation we *need* to maintain for the long term. It's not our client's job or anybody else's to keep us going. We need to provide ourselves with the initial motivation from our own criteria. Then we can enjoy those extras and bonuses because we don't desperately need them for our basic emotional sustenance. This is what makes it work!

After awhile in this business, I found I couldn't stay in this business if I had to just go from promotion to promotion. That wasn't enough. There had to be deeper reasons that would allow me to endure whatever challenges, hardships, disappointments, and frustrations came my way. With each hardship and disappointment, I found I needed even more than before. I wanted to come up with defense mechanisms and support systems that made it possible for me to live in a high rejection environment. Once my self-respect was inner-directed, I knew what I believed and what I had to offer. Then my quest became figuring out how to help others see the value of what I had.

THE PERSONAL BENEFITS OF OWNING YOUR OWN BUSINESS

When I talk about "personal integrity", I mean living by what you *believe* and what you *value*. Many people think of integrity only as honesty. Honesty towards others is a component of personal integrity—however much more as well. Personal integrity is not compromising what we believe because of an outside influence. It means being able to sleep at night because we've lived according to our own beliefs and values.

For many entrepreneurs, what drives them in business is their need and value for personal integrity—values that include creating situations where they won't have to compromise. There are many situations that may violate your standards, when you don't own your own business, with which you have to comply because you have a paycheck coming. You could live in a way that doesn't really line up with what you believe. This can create an internal conflict and a personal dilemma. We live a lower quality of life and we end up compromising ourselves for our paycheck. That says we're willing to sacrifice our values to meet our needs to get the paycheck.

A values conflict says this is not honest for me and it doesn't allow me to live without conflict on a daily basis. There are a lot of people who may go into business for themselves because they say, "I can't put up with this anymore, I can do this better."

THE E MYTH FACTOR

Then they leave their business and become a practitioner rather than an entrepreneur. They wear themselves out trying to be the chief cook and bottle washer. . . and everything else. Still, one of the main benefits of owning your own business is that you're able to make decisions and operate according to your own conscience and your own beliefs and values. You don't have to do what your CEO, sales manager, or supervisor tells you to do that could be in conflict with what you believe and what you stand for.

Rather than being run by the organization, hierarchy, or organizational chart, when we go into business for ourselves, we can live according to our conscience. We have an internal decision-making process that guides us rather than an externally driven process that creates a dilemma of values or beliefs for us. However, almost any experienced entrepreneur will agree that owning your own business is never a "piece of cake!" And going into business for yourself is never an acceptable way to avoid accepting responsibility in the workplace

Living by your conscience doesn't guarantee you'll automatically have the necessary skills to generate enough income to meet your needs. You could still starve to death—with a lot of integrity!

In *The E Myth*, Michael Gerber cites that once we decide we're going to live by our beliefs and values, we still have the responsibility to develop the skills required to accomplish the bottom line results we need to make it. We then have sufficient reason and motivation to sustain us during the time it takes to get the skills, gain the knowledge, and make it through.

When we work for somebody else, by default, we are in an external system that holds us accountable. You can say, "Well, I couldn't help it, they said I had to be there." When you own your own business, you have to switch that over to an internal system of accountability and self-discipline. Not everybody initially has the self-discipline required to launch a new business. It's one thing to have the skills, and another thing to be willing to do what's required to produce the bottom line results necessary for surviving and prospering.

No matter what the reason for going into your own business, there is an opportunity. It's not necessary to say, "I went into this for the wrong reason, so I guess I might as well go back to my old job, or forget it." Whether or not you were prepared internally with the willingness to succeed, or externally with the skills, getting the outcome you want is possible.

Whatever the reason, owning your own business still gives you the freedom to be self-determined by your own beliefs and values with the freedom and flexibility you need to live according to your conscience. I now have no excuse not to accept total responsibility for everything I think, say, do and feel, and to set my life up so that my dream has a chance to happen. What I do ultimately determines whether I'm successful or not.

What if, "Man does not live by values alone." Success is not only living by your conscience, you need to have the knowledge, skill, ability, and willingness to use your ability to create the outcomes you need for your survival and prosperity.

Accepting the responsibility is making the commitment to go your own way. Sometimes it is anger that initiates this and you say, "I don't want to live like this anymore." Or sometimes you say, "If I'm going to be honest with myself, I know that I don't want somebody that doesn't think, believe, or feel the way I do telling me what to do and how to run my life. The outcome I try to achieve is to live my life the way God tells me. If I'm honest, I know I don't always do what God tells me. So I'm surely not going to listen when you tell me how to run my life"!

If God gives a duck the sense to know when to fly south for the winter and He gives a bear the sense to hibernate, then He will also give me the sense to listen and tune in when I need to know where to go next in my life. It may take getting quiet, letting the roar of expectation and duty, the bills that need to be paid, and all these things, gradually die down in order to do some soul searching. We need to get quiet for a while, listen and tune in to our heart. Then we can find out if the direction we are taking is one that fits to combine meeting our basic needs, values, and beliefs together.

In today's business climate, "job security" is an out-of-date expression. A friend of mine worked for an Energy Corporation in Dallas for 19 years and was the VP of Human Resources. A little over a year ago, the company was sold. New management came in and old management went out. And my friend went out with the old management. After almost 20 years of working to build this company, he was out of a job and left thinking, "I'm 43 years old. Now what do I want to do with my life?"

With corporate downsizing, restructuring and outsourcing, getting your security from the company you work for—IBM, Citibank, Xerox or whatever—is an illusion. We've known for years that the only people who have true security are the ones with the skills and abilities to market themselves and generate their own income. If we're willing to do some new things—maybe even some things we don't like—we can better insure our success.

COMMITMENT

Once you've made your decision, you've committed to take action and you've done what you need for your project to succeed, there are going to be some issues, mentally and emotionally, that you may need to prepare for. If you don't deal with these issues, you may find the feedback you get from your environment might hook you into value judging (should, ought, or must). Or worse, someone could discourage you in such a way that you could give up on your new idea or your new direction before it has a chance to happen.

When you make an intellectual decision, you can ask yourself how you felt about your original decision and if you feel you made a wise choice. Most people will say they felt pretty sure about it. They also say they were pretty scared and excited! At the same time they are optimistic it will work out. Since they feel sure about their decision, they may believe friends and family will feel equally excited for them.

We picture ourselves walking in the door, the phones ringing, we pick up and hear, "We heard you got involved with that fine, fine company. Congratulations. This is wonderful. We've known for years what great potential you have and we know you're going to be enormously successful! Come over immediately, do your presentation, and let me look at your products and hear about your opportunity so I can be the first one to buy from you! I'll be able to say I knew you way back when you first got started."

Were this actually to happen, you might say, "I know this is just further confirmation and proof that I'm right in the middle of my own master plan, I've found my direction." You know this is exactly where you're supposed to be, there's no doubt in your mind and this new opportunity is where you're committed to spend the rest of your life and build your future.

For most people, this is *not* the way it happens! And what does normally happen? Often you begin to get feedback from other people saying, "You're in business for yourself? You, sell? You couldn't sell a raft to a drowning man. You've never sold before. Don't you remember back in high school when we were trying to raise money for new uniforms, you didn't sell one box of candy or one candle. You've never been able to sell! Don't get me wrong, we love you anyway, but you don't know what you're doing. You got a college education for this? You're wasting your life away. Are you going to become one of these manipulative, pushy salespeople who are trying to sell to their friends all the time?"

Whatever the scenario may be, you might go and sit on the edge of your bed or in your desk chair and put your head in your hands and say, "What have I done?" You may say to yourself, "Wait a minute. I forgot about that. I haven't sold. I can't sell. How did I let somebody talk me into this?"

Before you really jump into this wholeheartedly, maybe you need to do a little bit more research to be sure you didn't make an unwise choice. Maybe you need to go to another seminar or read another book, pray a bit more and make sure you're not making a big mistake here. It's possible to make a decision and still not have a commitment that allows you to take action. Because there's still a little question in the back of your mind.

BECOMING SINGLE-MINDED

In Latin, the root word for 'doubt' is 'dubare'. It means "to be divided in your mind," or "being pulled in two equal and opposite directions simultaneously." It's like having two boats—with your left foot in one boat and your right foot in another boat. While trying to decide which boat to jump into, you do the splits and hit the water!

Making a commitment is making a decision and allowing your divided mind to become a single mind firmly focused. When you are focused, it's critical to give yourself the time necessary for the learning to happen—even when people give you negative feedback, like, "This is a waste of time; you don't know what you're doing." Even though you know this was a wise choice based on how well you know yourself, most of us aren't sure how people will respond. We hope people are going to be happy for our decision—especially friends and family.

TRUSTING OUR DECISIONS

If people aren't supportive, we need to be able to trust our own decision.

One day, I was leaving the house when "The Price Is Right" came on the TV. (Even though I needed to get going, I lingered a minute in the doorway to just watch for a second!) One woman guessed the correct price of the item displayed and advanced to the next level on stage. She was so excited she was jumping up and down, hugging host Bob Barker! He announced, "Now, we're going to play the high-low game. You'll guess if the price showing is higher or lower than the actual retail price. If you guess correctly, you win this...a new car!" (music swells).

Even though she had guessed correctly on her own, now the stakes were higher so she turned to her husband for help. The crowd was yelling "higher" and her husband was yelling "lower." She was obviously torn. She looked again at her husband and the crowd– then back at the item. She looked at her husband for advice one last time and said, "lower." They lifted the price cover to reveal the answer and you guessed it. . . she lost. She didn't trust herself even though she had been successful the first time! And her lack of confidence in her own decision cost her the prize. Her poor husband probably never heard the end of it...*If you hadn't told me blah,blah,blah* . What is it that causes us to stop trusting ourselves inside on the big decisions?

When we go into a new business or venture, most people turn first to their family and friends for support. However, friends and family don't always provide the support we desire and often expect. Many times our family and friends are used to us behaving in a certain way; we are "boxed" into that limited role. Our family and friends are most comfortable when we are in that role. When we change, they may believe they will need to change too. By keeping us in a box, they protect themselves by not letting us go too far, or change too drastically.

What people are implying is, "Stay in this box. I don't want you to change because if you do, I'm going to have to change the way I deal with you. I know just exactly what to say to make you laugh, cry, or do something for me. If you change, I'll have to go back and figure this out all over again!" Like our family and friends, we may find our "box" comfortable as well. Our fear may be that when we begin to actually do what we're capable of doing, we will leave people behind, give up our current circle of friends, and maybe even start a whole new life. We don't want to leave anybody behind even though they may choose not to grow at the same time!

Yet, with the decision to move out of your box, you're able to say to yourself, "With all my gifts, talents and abilities, and with all the under-utilized potential I have, how can I justify the fact that this is as far as I'm going with what I've been given? 'One step below the angels' and I'm settling for the status quo, just surviving."

Here's where the dilemma begins. When you step out of the box and decide you're ready to do something, the closest people in your life may cry "Foul" and begin to "get concerned" about your new direction. They're in the same old place. They're still in their box.

They're going to want to keep you in this box if they can, not so much because they don't want you to grow, however because *they* don't want to grow. Or they could be fearful that you're going to grow off and leave them. The fact of the matter is if you don't grow, you'll die.

If we don't grow, I believe there's a hopelessness and a demoralization that can set in because the developmental process has been stopped.

There's something in us, whether it's an acorn wanting to become an oak tree, or us with our gifts and talents wanting to develop ourselves to the fullest. We want to become actualized and fulfilled as a person, to live life at its fullest.

When you know the business direction you chose was a decision made from an internal place and not an external place, you can justify continuing the growth process. The fact of the matter is the only way you know you are growing is if you observe yourself taking action and seeing it through to the end. When you keep up or increase your activity level by making the contacts and following through, you see that you are making progress. You're encouraged by seeing the changes that are taking place in your life; you're getting closer to fulfilling the dreams or outcomes you're after.

If we don't see the ongoing progress or refinement, we get discouraged and shut down.

EXPANDING OUR CIRCLE OF INFLUENCE

There's a profound book by Kaleel Jamison called *The Nibble Theory*. Jamison uses circles as a metaphor for learning and growth. We all have "a circle" and our circles get nibbled by other people when we hear discouraging comments. And people usually try to take a bite out of our circle, when we're trying to grow or expand our circle to its full capacity.

Nibbling comments may be things like, "You don't know what you're doing. You've never done anything like this before. This isn't like you. You're never going to make it. There's no way you're going to be able to do something like this." They keep nibbling away at your circle, which is their way of telling you they don't want you to grow bigger than their circle because then you are a threat to them.

When you make a commitment to yourself or begin to go your own way, your circle begins to expand!

Some people can't let their circle grow. They give in and don't let their circle expand to its potential. They don't ask for their missing pieces or for what they need to be healthy, not just for themselves, however for everyone involved. Jamison talks about what happens when we finally accept responsibility for allowing our circle to be its full size.

For example, say you have a person with a big circle and a person with a small circle. Instead of the big circle enlarging his circle at the expense of the small circle, the person with the small circle enlarges his circle to its full size. Then you have two, large fully-developed circles that have the potential to have two times the impact. That's the potential!

However, many of us don't find environments that encourage us to grow our circles to full capacity. Sometimes our close friends and family treat us in a more discouraging way than others. They sometimes fear we might fail so they attempt to protect us from even trying. Our friends or family think that if they can scare us out of trying then perhaps we won't get disappointed. That's one way friends and family try to help us.

Then there comes a time when we've developed to a point where our commitment has allowed us to know what we're doing is the correct direction for us. We can then go back in our environment, and the world will know that they're not going to shake our commitment. We let everybody else, and especially ourselves, know that we are committed to doing this, regardless of what we get externally. We have an internal drive and a commitment that's going to allow us to hang in and stay committed.

SETTLING THE ISSUE ONCE AND FOR ALL

If you would like to settle this issue, consider developing your skills and abilities to the degree where you can reach a level of credibility. Some of my clients in Direct Sales have cars as incentives. They say when they win the use of a new car as a part of their achievement level, they're tempted to drive that new free car by the people who doubted them to let them know they didn't give up. . .just to show them they had it in them to change and that they didn't quit. The fact is we don't need to do this for them; we want to do this for *us* so we can move on to the next level and not settle for less.

FINDING REASONS TO KEEP A COMMITMENT

I'm reminded of a story I heard told by a missionary who had been in China. He saw an elderly Chinese man along the side of the road. The man was suffering from malnutrition, blind from cataracts, and had fallen into a ditch and was dying there. The missionary scooped him up and took him to a clinic a few miles away where he was nursed back to health.

They were even able to perform eye surgery and remove his cataracts so he could see.

The man was so grateful since he believed he was going to die that he committed the rest of his life to helping other people find the clinic so they could get the same kind of help he'd gotten. He went to the surrounding villages and found people who couldn't see and needed help. Then the man took a length of rope and tied a knot in one end of it. Then, he built a carrying device with the rope. He said, "Hold on to the rope and I'll show you where you can get help. I know they can help because I wouldn't be alive today if it weren't for them."

It's unfortunate, that sometimes friends have a hold on us because they know we've given up on ourselves before and they won't let us forget it. They think this is just another one of those "fads" that will pass.

The principle is, after you learn what you need and get the skills you need, then you develop your ability to create the outcome. Once you've taken care of yourself and have the credibility of experience, you can go back into the box and you can talk to anybody. They'll know you've got the persistence, the ability to bounce back, the mental, emotional, and spiritual wherewithal and commitment to stick to your direction. You'll be impervious to negative nibbling because you'll be established on sound footing. You'll also have convinced yourself that you're sticking with this and you're going to see it through to the end.

THE CHALLENGE

The world is full of small-minded

people content with where they are,

not knowing the joys success could bring

and no will to go that far.

Would you be one who dares try

when challenged by a task

to rise to heights you've never seen,

or is that too much to ask?

This is your day, a world to win

and great purpose to achieve.

Accept the challenge of your goals

and in yourself believe.

You'll be pleased at what you've done

when at the close of day

you can look back on all these battles won,

content you went ahead and came that way.

Hartsill Wilson

The movie "The Karate Kid" is a great example of this. The wise old Mr. Myagi is confronted by the young boy Daniel. Daniel wants the old master to teach him karate after some neighborhood kids stole his bicycle and beat him up. When he asked Mr. Myagi to teach him karate, the old man replied, "I am not willing to be your teacher unless you do as I say, no questions asked, a total commitment. Nothing less will do. If you are a grape on left side of road, that okay. If you are a grape on right side of road, that okay too. If you are a grape in middle of road, squish. Daniel-san, if you are going to be in, be in. If you are going to be out, be out. If you are in the middle. . . squish."

The consequences of being "neither hot nor cold" leave you open to falling prey to nibblers. Whatever commitment you've made, your direction, realize that if you are in, you need to be in, and if you are going to be out, be out. Don't be in the middle acting like your 'in' when you're not. And don't be in the middle acting like your 'out' when you're not.

If we have a divided mind, a divided focus, or we don't have a singleness of purpose, then we don't have the kind of commitment that would allow us to see through the question marks and the doubts that are nibbling us from other people.

BELIEVE IT, THEN SEE IT

I once had the great opportunity to meet and hear Wally "Famous Amos" tell the story of how he started his cookie business.

"Famous Amos" made a commitment to his business before it began. For about two months, before he had even baked one cookie, he told people that he had started a cookie business! His friends told him to quit telling people this because he had no equipment, no place to make cookies, and he had no cookies! They told him people would think he was crazy. "Famous Amos," quite frankly, told them to leave him alone; he would start the business and all the rest would come.

Then he got a call one day from one of his friends who said, "I'm sitting here with a banker. He's got some equipment he's repossessed and he's got warehouse space. He's willing to do business if you're serious about this cookie thing. If you're serious, you need to come down and talk to this guy because he can actually help you make this happen!"

He went to meet with the banker and the rest is history.

Later on after his business was off and running, "Famous Amos" told his friend, "Well, if he wasn't the one to help me get my business launched, it would have been somebody else." He knew that you believe it first, and then you see it. It's not the other way around.

TIDDLYWINKS

There is a Tiddlywinks® tournament held every year and the grand prize is $200,000! This proves that no matter what you do, you can be the best and you can do well. If you're pursuing being the best at your life's direction, you'll find what you need.

It's sad to know there are doctors that would probably have been more satisfied in other healing professions. They may have become an acupuncturist or a massage therapist and had a lifestyle that was more to their liking. Or that there are attorneys who would have been more satisfied being writers. Whatever the profession or service, there are people today who are dissatisfied with their lives and are settling for much less than they deserve.

The marketplace today is beginning to swell with people who are starting their own small cottage industry, personal business, out of their home using whatever product or service is a fit for them. They want their business to grow into something big, to allow them to live according to their beliefs and values, and have more flexibility and freedom. They want to maintain their own standards, or lifestyle, or have more of what they want and not settle for less. Part of finding your direction is looking at yourself and seeing if you're "off course" and can redirect. Redirection is *always* possible.

The idea is that you don't have to stop doing what you're doing, Start doing what you need, to be able to give yourself room (and a chance) to grow.

LIFE DECISIONS

I heard Keith DeGreen share a story about two men sitting on a park bench thinking back about the way they'd invested their life, and one of them said, "I can remember back when I could have gone ahead and done this or that, taken a certain job, could have gone ahead and taken that class, got my education. I remember the times when I could have done it, yet you know, now it seems like so many decisions I made didn't total up to what I wanted my life to be."

And then the person next to him said, "You know, I sure am glad I did those things, because I know what you're talking about. And it wasn't easy— let me tell you, those decisions that you chose not to make, I almost didn't make them either. I know that, because I went ahead and endured the sacrifice and did it, I know that's the reason my life's so rich right now. I know it's the reason I'm getting the payoff that I am, and it was no accident. It wasn't easy, however I sure am glad I did it."

These are the kinds of decisions you're making every single day. Are you going to postpone the outcomes? Are you going to sabotage your success until the time slips away? Or, are you going to go ahead and take action on what you have a chance to do now?

MY WAGE

I bargained with life for a penny

but life would pay no more,

and then I begged at evening

when I counted my scanty store,

for life is a just employer

and it pays you what you ask.

However, once you set the wage,

you have to bear the task.

I work for a menial's hire

and then I learned, dismayed,

that whatever wage I would have asked of life,

life gladly would have paid.

Jessie B. Rittenhouse

FOOD FOR THOUGHT

- How could you accept responsibility for everything you think, say, do and feel?

- How do your choices determine the outcomes you experience and the direction your life will take?

- In what way is experiencing the consequences of your behavior an opportunity for personal growth?

- What can you do to help yourself and others meet their basic needs?

- In what meaningful way can you support others emotionally, giving them total unconditional acceptance?

- What circumstances would need to exist for you to deepen your personal commitment to your chosen direction?

- Is it worth it to branch off and become your own person? What makes it worthwhile?

CHAPTER 5

Leaves

What do we know about leaves on a tree? In the autumn, they turn vibrant colors just before they fall. Does this mean the tree has died? No, we know the leaves return in the spring!

My oldest daughter, Katie, was about four when we were sitting in the spa watching leaves fall off the trees in our backyard. Some of the leaves were floating down and landing in the water. She said sadly, "Daddy, the leaves are dying." I said, "They'll only be gone for the winter, honey, so the tree won't have to feed them and the tree can rest awhile. They'll be back in the spring when the flowers start to bloom." She looked relieved and said "Oh, OK!"

Like the tree, it is okay to replace our old patterns to encourage new, healthy growth. This cycle is part of every phase of our lives. Do you have issues in your life that return regularly (for example: financial stress, conflict in your relationships, feeling pressured and not having enough time, or chronic health concerns) that need to be replaced with new growth? When we make a serious commitment to fulfill our dream (or "branch off" and use our uniqueness to find our direction) recurrent barriers may become obvious. If we don't address these issues, we simply don't have hope that we can move ahead and take action to live the dream of our new direction.

A number of years ago, I had the opportunity to study under Dr. Edith Stauffer, author of the book *Unconditional Love and Forgiveness*. She blends philosophy from the ancient Essenes (Jesus grew up as an Essene and their philosophy is found within the Sermon on the Mount) with Roberto Asagioli's concept of Psycho-synthesis (life patterns). My interaction with Dr. Stauffer produced a life changing insight for me.

At a conference, Dr. Stauffer, who was close to eighty and extremely vibrant, asked us to think back to when we were around three years old and remember how our needs were met. Then we began to identify repeating patterns in our life, using a dialog that allowed us to confront our sub-personalities.

I remembered that I was a little boy who wanted to be loved and recognized. I would get attention by helping and being funny. Guess what, I still do that today! To avoid criticism and make sure I didn't disappoint anyone (especially my parents, pastor, teachers and other authority figures), I would sometimes "martyr" myself by over-giving or put other people's needs ahead of my own, in an unhealthy manner. Oftentimes, I would find I was burned out emotionally because I hadn't considered myself and my needs while I was busy giving to others.

There is a fine line between caring for and serving others unselfishly and going overboard. You cross the line when you begin giving to the point where there's nothing left to give *anyone.* Unhealthy self-sacrifice is inwardly driven by using over-giving as a way to "justify" yourself. If you engage in exhaustive over-giving as a means of providing relief from guilt, you are participating in unhealthy activity.

Next, Dr. Stauffer asked us to think about the patterns that carried over from our childhood into our adult life. She noted that when we were three years old we met our needs, using our limited coping skills. If we are still using these coping patterns today (and they are not working), it's like attempting to wear a pair of size 2 shoes that fit us as a three-year-old when we now wear a size 9 as an adult. Can you imagine how uncomfortable it would be trying to tiptoe around in a pair of shoes fit for a toddler?

In Dr. Stauffer's class, we began to explore ways to address our unhealthy patterns. The process began with a dialogue with ourselves designed to empower us to address the unhealthy patterns. I raised myself to my full height and said, "I'm Bill and I'm in charge and I want to know the reason you want me to over-give all the time?" Then, at Dr. Stauffer's direction, I switched to play the role of the Martyr. With my hands outstretched as in offering support, the Martyr responded, "You need me to make sure you give enough."

I firmly asked, "Where does this come from and where did it begin?" The Martyr reminded me of a time when I was eight or nine and felt lazy. I believed God, my parents, and everyone I knew was disappointed with me. I wasn't doing "enough."

When I asked the Martyr the reason it wouldn't leave, it said, "You need me. I protect you. If you don't give enough, what will people do if you don't help them: They'll suffer. It's all up to you. And you know, people may not love you if you stop giving so much."

At that moment, I realized the motivation that had been driving me for so long.

I stood even taller than before and said, "Thank you for trying to help me and protect me all these years. Now I no longer feel the need to martyr myself unnecessarily. It's time for you to go. I will still give and serve others, however starting now, I will allow myself to have what I need as well." The Martyr's voice was faint as it informed me it would leave for now yet stay close in case I needed it to rush back in to help me give "enough."

"Thank you," I said, "I'll be fine."

This revealed an "overly helpful inner friend" that I didn't even know I had for close to thirty years. These patterns don't leave or change easily. However, they will change when we determine to replace patterns that are not working with healthier patterns that do work for us.

Being a martyr was my issue. There are other issues that may come out: the victim, the critic, the helper, the cynic, the do-gooder, the timid soul, the procrastinator, etc. What are your reoccurring barriers? Are you ready to let go of them? Can you justify staying where you are now—if the choice is between the pain of growth or the pain of staying the same? What would it take to make growth valuable to you? If a tree doesn't produce new leaves, chances are it's dead. It we don't grow beyond our old patterns, part of us dies—our hope for the future. Continual growth allows you to move ahead in your chosen direction.

GIVING AND RECEIVING

We all grew up in places

We heard our elders say

Tis more blessed to give than to receive

Yes, it's the only way

So that receiving was the enemy

To guard against, no doubt

But receiving plays an important part

Of how our life turns out

We feel comfortable in the martyr role

Suffering through our lonely ordeal

We would rather act as if it's fine

Than let on how we feel

Sometimes we will say "thanks anyway, don't bother",

And then die as they walk away

"Are you thirsty?"

"No, I'm fine", as we swallow hard

For that's the thing to say

What is the shame as a human being

To have an occasional need

To say "Yes, thank you so"

And allow others a kindness received

Yes, giving is a blessing, and it fills our hearts with joy,

But if we can't receive one too,

It may just be a controlling ploy.

If we do all the giving, though

And keep the blessing for our own

How can we call ourselves true givers, then

Until the blessing's known?

We want the other person to feel

The joy that giving brings

So learn to receive in such a way

That it allows another giving heart to sing

Now with this lesson learned

We can ask for our missing piece

Our yes will mean yes,

Our no will mean no

And this dishonest game will cease.

Bill Cantrell

GROWTH AND CHANGE

Growth and change go hand in hand. Is it possible we slow down our growth and development, as we find our direction, in order to prevent things from getting overwhelming? Learning to change and grow without holding back could help us move ahead faster.

Linda Sasha, a colleague in the training business, has a creative way of using Jenssen's change model to help people through the change process.

Change is inevitable like the seasons. The seasons change whether we are ready or not. Change is the season's predictable quality. What if we approached life like the seasons? Like the tree grows from seeds into roots, trunk, branches, leaves and fruit, there is a process to life growth that happens by design.

THE COMFORT ZONE PHASE

The first stage is comfort zone and it is like the summer when living is easy. Sometimes we linger a bit too long in our summertime mentality before getting back to "school" (learning and growth).

THE DENIAL PHASE

Stage two is denial and it comes in the fall. You know summer's not over—this is Indian summer. Maybe the wind is blowing, the leaves are falling, but we're still hanging on to our summer. The time to grow and move on with our life has long since past.

Moving through the Denial phase requires grieving our losses. These would include disappointments in business or relationships, people we have heavily invested in that don't pan out, or hard-earned money and time invested in a project that goes under. If we aren't careful, these memories of painful disappointments could prevent us from moving on if we decide to protect ourselves from the same disappointment happening again. We need to acknowledge our feelings of sadness, disappointment, or frustration, realize they are justified and we need to feel them fully...then move on.

Change is a natural part of growing. If we don't grow, we begin to die. Mike Vance, former dean of Disney University, said, "People aren't afraid of changing and growing. They're afraid they won't change enough."

In their book, *Forgiveness*, co-authors Sidney B. Simon and Suzanne Simon list six stages we move through on the way to acceptance and integration of painful events into the whole of our lives.

Denial: "It happened so long ago, everything is just fine."

Self-Blame: "Maybe I set it up, maybe I asked for it."

Victim: "Because I was a victim, don't expect too much from me."

Indignation: Bold, justified anger with a tendency to generalize. For example, generalizing with phrases like: all men or women are like this.

Survivor: "I have made it through; looking back, I guess they did the best they could at the time." Sense of humor begins to return.

Integration: "I am ready to fit this event or this situation into the whole of my life; I am more than this one experience. What lessons can I gain from having experienced this?"

Not unlike Elizabeth Kubler-Ross' stages in *Death and Dying*, the Simons show that we need some time to grieve our losses—to list them, feel the feelings and let them go.

THE CONFUSION PHASE

Jenssen calls the next stage Confusion. Confusion is the winter and is also what people most resist. If you have ever moved from one home to another and had all your possessions in boxes or if you've had a renovation project done on your existing home, you know what confusion feels like.

To move out of confusion, we need to accept responsibility for redesigning our life. We need to actively participate in the change, because it does not happen on its own. At this stage, it is important to stop and review what you need, want, and value. Clarify your ideal outcomes then begin participating in the change process.

THE RENEWAL PHASE

We can then leave the winter and enter the renewal phase of spring. This is the celebration time. The change has been made. Our joy is then in direct proportion to our participation in the redesigning of our lives and circumstances. This is not the end because we will move into the Comfort Zone cycle again. We will repeat this cycle many times in different areas of our lives.

CHANGING OUR DAILY HABIT PATTERNS

Once we accept responsibility for change, we need to evaluate our daily habits. A part of the brain (the reticular activating system) is designed in such a way that when we plant and reinforce an idea as if we have already accomplished it, we will notice people or circumstances begin to help making it a reality.

Here is an example of how this concept works: Did you ever buy a new car? You probably didn't notice many cars like it on the road until you got yours. Then similar cars seemed to be everywhere! Or perhaps you've bought a new outfit and see someone else with one exactly like it the same day. You probably wouldn't have noticed the other person's outfit until you got the identical outfit. When I was in college, I grew a beard and I thought everyone on campus grew a beard. They hadn't, yet now I just noticed every beard on campus!

Our vision may clear after we decide to make our new direction a reality. The necessary tools for the accomplishment may have always been present; we just did not realize it until we were ready to make the commitment.

A strong level of commitment requires language such as, "I'm going to believe this is happening even before it happens. I know that everything I see and do is reflective of that. I will find all the ingredients I need along the way."

Have you noticed if you're a worrier, that even though you don't have anything to do, your mind will just automatically worry for you? Building a new habit is a challenge. We don't like to change. There's going to be some initial resistance, but if we go ahead and push through the pain and complete the change, the payoff will last a lifetime.

Maxwell Maltz says it takes twenty-one days to build a new habit. For example, if you move your wastepaper basket to the right side of your desk from the left, you will throw paper on the floor for three weeks. It will take time to form a new habit. You can either begin reinforcing the desired habit or keep reinforcing the old one. I don't know if it's going to be worth it to you to change your habits. At least, open yourself up to changing habits that create new outcomes. These new outcomes will happen one layer at a time.

You don't even have to think about old habits because you've done them for so long. It is second nature to continue doing things the same way you always have done them. It is more comfortable to stay with the old habits even when you know learning a new habit will give you a better outcome. You may be stressed emotionally or financially. If you know learning a new behavior will help you, you need to begin to practice now.

I can't promise you changing habits will be easy. It's never been easy for me. It's always been worth it. I still have many areas that I'm continuously working on, and every habit I work on gives me a more positive outcome than I had before I made the attempt to change.

You can spend your whole life thinking about making a change. It's possible that you could find yourself down the road ten, fifteen, or twenty years from now saying to yourself, "I knew better than to let this happen. I can't believe how quickly the years have gotten away. I've ended up just going ahead and doing it the way I've always done it. Yet, I know I could have had more. It seems like I ate the peeling and threw the banana away."

For me, it is important that I don't live too much of my life not making changes that could have provided a different outcome for me and the people I care about.

A BUILDER'S LESSON

How shall I a habit break?

As you did that habit make.

As you gathered, you now loose;

As you yielded, now refuse.

Thread by thread the strands we twist

Till they bind us, neck and wrist.

Thread by thread the patient hand

Now untwines, ere free we stand.

As we builded, stone by stone,

We now toil, unhelped, alone,

Till the wall is overthrown.

John Boyle O'Reilly

PREVENTING PROCRASTINATION

There are many reasons for putting things off. However, there are two main reasons for procrastination: Number one is Perfectionism. Have you ever dealt with perfection? Do you procrastinate because you can't get the job done just right? Have you ever said to yourself, "I'm going to wait until I can do this well. Anything worth doing is worth doing well."? Can we get hooked by perfectionism? Sure. Perfectionism is placing a higher priority on getting things done correctly than doing the correct thing. We can do something perfectly and it doesn't necessarily make a contribution to the outcomes we're after. I think that people often perfect things of little consequence rather than doing something consequential and doing it well.

We need to align our priorities with our chosen life direction. It is possible for a person, starting their business, to get a new inventory order in—and tied up in perfectionism—unpack their order from the company, get it up on the shelf, take their ruler making sure the boxes are about one inch from the edge of the shelf, and make sure all the boxes are lined up with the labels forward. Then one of their customers calls to place an order and the person goes through their shelf, thinking, "Awww, it's going to leave this great big gaping hole right here!" What are you in business for? This is what Peter Drucker calls efficiency. Efficiency is when you do things the correct way, and then the other side is effectiveness. That's doing the correct, most productive thing. Doing the correct activity produces results.

Now, what is the correct thing to do? Where do you make your money in your business? When do you build the relationships in your business? With face-to-face, eyeball-to eyeball contact with people. If you bury yourself in your kitchen, your office or someplace, and hide out from the world and memorize your Business guide, hoping and praying that people will call you, and that maybe a neighbor will tell somebody what you are doing, you will not get the same outcome as if you are getting involved in your community, building a network, investing your life in your church, school, friends, neighbors, selling and recruiting, and telling others about what you do. Do you think it would be hard to keep your business from growing? I think it would. There is no way that you can keep your business from growing if you're investing like that. If you spend time with people in the community (doing the effective thing), you have more time to do things as well as you can.

I grew up with perfectionism. My mother used to say, "We are not going anywhere until the kitchen is clean." I would reply, "Mom, this is the biggest game of the year. Aw, mom, everybody's waiting on us." She would reply, "You all get in there and you clean up that kitchen right now. Get that kitchen clean!"

I didn't always know the reason it was important to my mother and I chose to resist it at the time. I didn't think it was as important as she did, because I wanted to do the fun thing. I wanted to go to the ball game and see everybody, or whatever the event happened to be. There are some things that we need to do well. We need to balance and know that when we have the time to perfect things, it is okay. However, most of us don't have time to do things perfectly, so if we can learn to settle for the best we can do with the time we have, and then get on with it, a lot more of us would cover a lot more ground. What if you give yourself permission to make mistakes then take action?

LOW FRUSTRATION TOLERANCE

After perfectionism comes low frustration tolerance (LFT). Most of us don't like to do what we don't like to do. We do like to do what we like to do. Logically, we spend most of our time doing what we like to do. If we have a choice, we usually do what we like to do. We have the freedom to choose. Though it may not always give us the desired outcome, we settle for what it gives us anyway.

We actually have two choices. We can live how we want to live, settling for the outcome, or we can decide on the outcome that we want and do whatever it takes to get that outcome. We work from one choice or the other. Low frustration tolerance means that there are many things we choose not to do simply because it's too much of a hassle. We say to ourselves "A person doesn't need to do anymore than what we are doing to become successful. This is enough already." Is it possible you and I don't realize that what we've done may only be a fraction of what it actually takes? People throughout history have realized that it actually takes much more than most of us think to get the necessary things accomplished. We say, "No, I've done enough."

Who knows, maybe one of these days I will wake up one morning, kick a big paper sack full of money on the way to the grocery store and never have to work hard again. I could just go to the Bahamas and hang out. Or, you know I have that well-to-do distant relative that has more money than she lets on. Nobody can live forever. You never know, one of these days I could get an inheritance check. How many of us dream about these things rescuing us so that we can quit going through all the hassle of making ends meet? We dream that, one of these days, some miracle out of the sky is going to fall and we won't have to work anymore. These thoughts come through my mind, but let me share a lesson my father taught me. My dad owned his own business. One day, in the back of the warehouse, I asked, "Dad, do you like doing this inventory? Man that paperwork looks boring! How do you do all that?" He said, "No, son, it's just one of those things that has to be done. If you're going to own your own business its important for your success so you just do it." Then he said, "Get back to work."

It "just needs to be done" if you want a particular outcome. Now, if you don't want the outcome it doesn't make any difference. Just adjust what you will settle for. For instance, we have a monster exam in school. This exam is a third of our grade, so I go home and say I'm really going to study this time. Sunday night at nine o'clock I hop in bed, pull the covers up to my waist, surround myself with a two-liter Dr. Pepper and a big bowl of pretzels, and turn on the TV to settle in for a long night of high-performance studying.

Based on my behavior, what do I really want to do? I want to play and watch TV. During the commercials, I flip through a textbook (sometimes the commercials are more interesting and I watch them instead). I begin to feel a little drowsy, so I say to myself, "History! I'm never going to remember all of these dates! What I need to do is get some sleep and get up early to study." So, I drift off to sleep and wake up with the birds chirping in the bright sunshine. I forgot to set the alarm. I rush to class. During the exam, we all pray the same prayer: "Lord, if you'll just help me get some of these answers, I promise. . . ." Thank goodness, it's multiple choice or we wouldn't even have a prayer.

It sounds crazy, yet it's not as crazy as what actually happens. We start believing that we actually get the ability and the power to figure the answers out even though we didn't study. We start saying things like, "None of these look familiar, but this answer looks a little friendlier. Yes, it just looks like the answer." We start picking a few of these, confidence starts growing, and we are getting out of control. We know we won't ace the test, yet we expect to squeak by with a 68. About the middle of the test we begin to think maybe we will make a 75. By the time we turn the test in, there is no telling, we think we will make an 80. A week later the teacher returns the test. We open it to find a 32! We think, "No way! How could I have made a 32? I know I guessed more of the answers than that! There is no way!"

Is it possible we deceive ourselves? Is it possible we could look across at a business colleague, associate, or friend and say, "I know for a fact they're not any better at their business than I am. How do they have those high selling weeks and great meetings? I know I could do everything he or she does because I'm just as competent as they are. What do they have that I don't?" Is there something we don't know? Is there any way you can know the thought process of another individual? Is there any way you can know how to measure persistence, perseverance, follow-up, and responsibility? We don't know these things until we really get to know somebody. Instead, we stand back at a distance and say, "I'm not getting my fair share. I'm doing just as much as everybody else and it's not happening for me."

In reality, we are not getting the job done. We are procrastinating, not realizing there is much more work than we're willing to do. We're saying, "I'm willing to do this much and that is it. I'll tell you there are some things in my business that if you saw me doing you would say, "He does that? You mean I have to do that?" No, only if you want the same outcome.

If you do want the outcome, don't put any limitations on what it will take because you might set limitations a lot lower than what is actually required. We might hope the world will respond anyway, but it doesn't work like that. Low frustration tolerance means that the requirements need to be non-negotiable commitments for us. We need to stop hoping that it will happen even if we are not willing to pay the price and do the work.

Sacrifice (Investment) ÷ Time = Payoff There's a little exercise that you can do. Sacrifice or investment and time are the components. For the purposes of evaluation, think about what success means to you. Do you think about lifestyle, financial security, travel, independence, or recognition? The question about success makes you think about what? Rewards. We focus on what we want, not what we need to give to get what we want. We think about the big payoff, yet it actually doesn't have anything to do with the ingredients we need to provide in order to make the payoff possible. What if you shifted your focus from 90% looking toward the rewards to 90% looking at the investment in preparation?

What if your mind was tied up into building and nurturing the investment ingredients that you need such as discipline, commitment, persistence, planning, follow-up, and work ethic? What if we switch over to start thinking about the investment we are going to make?

What about the time line? Is it possible for some people in the course of five years, for example, to push through all this sacrifice, growth, and investment in a short period of time to reach the payoff faster? Is it possible to take fifteen years? We can choose how much and how fast we want to accomplish something. One person says, "Well, it took me fifteen years because I have five children." The person who accomplished the goal in five years says, "I know what you mean, I have eight children." Your excuses are taken away. It is a choice.

If you go too fast and lose the values that are important to you, family or otherwise, you compromise your self-esteem. If you take too long, not getting your gifts and talents out to the world, you don't find out what you are capable of doing. You compromise your self-esteem. It is your choice.

I believe we need to find a balance somewhere in-between that works for us. A balance of not procrastinating, doing first things first, and getting your gifts and talents out without resisting what we have yet to do. Is the self-esteem issue holding you back? Are you waiting until you feel like you deserve your desired outcome? Are you telling yourself that you will act when it's time? I want today to bring you closer to saying, "Now is the time." Now is the time, so go ahead and do it.

RELEASING NEGATIVITY

When you were growing up, were there comments that shaped your life?

Did you experience negative comments that caused you pain? Such as: *"You're stupid. I hate you. Why can't you be more like your brother or sister? You always embarrass us."*

Were there also positive comments that caused us to feel wonderful? Did you hear words like: *"I love you. You are so special. I appreciate your friendship. I know you can do it."*?

Our interpretation of comments we labeled negative may have impacted us more than we realize.

Many people look back on their lives and realize that they have received more negative than positive comments. They were unable to accurately assess their value. Documented research by Shad Helmstetter states, 77% of the messages we receive while growing to adulthood are perceived as negative or non-affirming. This research also supports the fact that it takes ten affirming thoughts to cancel the effects of one negative comment or action.

If you ever had a painful or traumatic experience, like falling out of a tree and breaking your arm, you remember almost everything. The events leading up to the fall, the people who were there and what they said. On the other hand, can you remember who attended the birthday party or other nice things that happened to you that same year? Maybe not. The intensity of the painful experience anchored the memory on a deeper level.

We have a tremendous responsibility to guard our heart and mind and discipline our thoughts. What if we daily monitored the friends we spend time with, the music we listen to, the books we read, and our actions, to better insure that we are focusing on messages that reinforce the direction we have chosen.

However, neither the positives nor the negatives are accurate in determining who we are as a human being. For instance, if you went to a party and a person walked up to you and said, "What are you doing here. If I had known you were going to be here, I wouldn't have come to this. I can't stand even being in the same room with you. If you're staying, I'm leaving." You might think to yourself "What could I have done to make them so angry with me? I don't ever want anyone to be that upset with me." Then you turn right around and run into a close friend who says, "I'm so glad you're here. You're the best friend a person could ever have. You don't know this, however when you took time to listen the other day, you saved my life. You will never know the difference you've made." You give them a big hug and think to yourself, "Who Am I?" Which person am I?"

The responses of others does not necessarily reflect who we are. Nobody can evaluate you with 100% accuracy.

Others' words *do* reflect the current self-esteem level of the *sender.* Many of the comments we receive—and potentially take personally—are really the result of the hurting compromised self-esteem of the sender. Often, this is how self-esteem issues are transferred from one generation to the next.

No one ever knows all the facts. They don't know us, or the situation, well enough to know if they're on target. We visualize that people know all of the worst fears that we believe about ourselves. Then when somebody is non-affirming toward us we fear they are close enough to see deep inside of us. Sometimes these observations can be on target. If they do hit home, say *thank you!* (How many people have the courage, or even pay enough attention to us, to give us honest feedback and help us see our blind spots?)

We can't take feedback very well when our heart is broken, we're hurting, and life has dealt us a series of challenges. We don't have a chance to catch a breath or even get our head above water. We feel like we're drowning. When the world deals us too many of these events, we need a way to surround ourselves with protection. We then need to figure out if it's our issue (meaning the feedback is truth-based) or if it's *them*.

We go through difficult times; it doesn't mean we don't have people who love us or we don't have any positive affirmation left. However sometimes it pales in comparison to the engulfing quantity of life experiences we're not prepared to handle!

When a person feels mentally and emotionally healthy and has their self-esteem intact, they have a greater capacity to affirm others. Precisely because they were affirming, we know they were in a state of mind to give.

Let go of the affirming or non-affirming feedback you get from other people. Take both with a grain of salt and then let it go.

THREE-STEP PROCESS

At a lecture series I attended early in my career, my mentor's son Bill McGrane III, a close friend and colleague, shared an idea that helps me deal with feedback from others. Here's a simple, healthy three-step process you can use to protect yourself.

Step One:

If somebody gives you a non-affirming "hook" and tries to make you feel inadequate, look back at them and think:

"Cancel, cancel, I choose not to accept that."

Don't say it out loud—it'll confuse them!

Mary McDowell, a wise old sage from back in the hills of Tennessee, used to say, "It's OK for a bird to fly over your head, yet it's not OK for it to build a nest in your hair." You can hear these, non-affirming comments, yet you don't want to give them a place to stay for any length of time! Just because somebody says something hurtful, you don't need to accept it. Protect your inner core by tempering the comment and diffusing its potential harm.

Step Two:

After you've said, "cancel, cancel," ask yourself: "How are they feeling about *themselves* if they need to hurt me with what they say?" In his book *Born Only Once,* Conrad Barrs said "We can only affirm others up to the level we have been affirmed." If we don't begin the affirmation process with them, they may never receive it.

Remember, we don't have to accept their comments as truth. Their harmful comments can actually remind us to think about them and recognize that they could be hurting in some way.

Step Three:

The last step is where we can not only help them, we can turn the tide on the impact of what they've said. Ask yourself, "What can I say to help *them* feel better about who they are?" Often, we can meet the needs of someone who is hurting.

The steps are "Cancel, cancel, I choose not to accept that. How are they feeling about themselves? What can I say to help them feel better about themselves than they're feeling now? How can I affirm them?"

HANDLING THE "GROUCHES" IN OUR LIFE!

You're checking out at the grocery store, and a friend standing in line behind you sarcastically says, "I've heard you've started a new business. Made your big sale yet?"

You respond, "Well, I've only been in a short time, I'm enjoying the people and I'm learning a lot." Then you grab your groceries and run for your car. As you're leaving, you think, "I'm not sure I'll ever even make a big sale. Not only have I not made a big sale, I haven't made that many little sales either! Everybody said they weren't interested."

So what if you jump in your car, grab your steering wheel, grit your teeth and drive home, saying things like, "I can't believe I've been such a 'blithering idiot,' It was 'stupid' to think I could try to start my own business. I'm never going to get anywhere with this!"

After that kind of an experience, making calls to prospective clients is the last thing you want to do. If you believe what you have been telling yourself, you will not do anything to support what you think is a big mistake.

Your whole day could be impacted and it began at the grocery store! One cutting sarcastic remark can blow the whole day.

Here's an alternative scenario:

You've met a friend at the grocery store and she sarcastically says, "I've heard you've started a new business. Made your big sale yet?"

Instead of running, this time mentally say, "Cancel, cancel, I choose not to accept that. I wonder how she's feeling about herself since she needs to ridicule me? I wonder what I can say to help her feel a little bit better about her situation? What better opportunity do I have to share in a way she can modify her behavior?"

So you say, "You know, it's funny you say that because while we've been standing here, it crossed my mind how effective you'd be at sales. Even though I haven't made a big sale *yet*, I'm on target to get the outcome I want. Someone with your gifts and talents could be producing results like mine in just a short while. Would you like to hear how this works and how it could make a difference to you?"

Now how's she going to feel? Initially, she may be uncomfortable because you didn't produce the response expected. You didn't get hooked. You didn't say, "You know, I'm getting really sick and tired of you making wise cracks about my business." (That kind of comeback *really* helps the situation, doesn't it?) Instead, you showered her with kindness! So your friend says to herself, "She has always been nice to me, I don't know how come I have to be so mean. I wonder if there might be something to this new business of theirs?"

Since you have been genuinely kind to her, you may gain a new customer or even a new business associate. Whatever the timing, when she's ready, you'll be there for the payoff! The real bonus is how you feel when you walk out of the store. You pick up your groceries and as you leave you say to yourself, "What a great feeling. I can't believe I responded to her the way I did!"

You're cruising home, whistling, and you're thinking to yourself, "You know, even with one little adjustment in how I respond to negativity, I see growth that's taking place in me. If these kinds of things are happening now, I can only imagine what would happen if I really got serious about doing this business of mine! What I need to do when I get home is to get on the phone and make some phone calls. I know I've got a lot of people to contact." The rest of the day becomes incredibly productive!

When you're able to sensibly handle discouraging comments, you're able to give back a positive affirmation based on your chosen response and not on *their* behavior. Their behavior is saying, "I need more love and attention. I need more encouragement. I need you to affirm me."

Many people have never understood how "turning the other cheek" works. Yet, when we respond by returning negative for negative we only add to the problem. Instead, we can help someone heal by reinforcing their self-esteem if we're prepared to give an affirming word, *regardless* of what we receive from them.

Cavett Robert tells a story about growing up in Starkville, Mississippi, around the turn of the century. He remembered walking with his grandfather along the wooden sidewalks. His granddad would tip his hat to all the women in town as they passed by. When his grandfather tipped his hat to one woman, another woman in the town confronted him saying, "With her reputation, how dare you tip your hat to her as if she's a lady!"

Cavett's grandfather tipped his hat once again saying, "I beg your pardon, ma'am. I don't tip my hat to you because you're a lady. I tip my hat to you because I'm a gentleman."

Anybody who's genuinely feeling accepted is open, encouraging, and constantly affirming. Many times, these are people that can't find enough nice things to say and are caring enough to point out something we need to change. The sincere way in which the suggestion is phrased makes us glad they brought it to our attention.

If the same insight were given by someone with a personal agenda, who's smug or self-righteous, we might respond, "You've got no right to tell me how to live my life—how dare you! Knowing all that I know about you, how could you try to fix me?"

It's in the appropriateness of the language! We respond differently when we know the person cares. If we love and affirm the person, not the behavior—and give them the benefit of the doubt—people can change and miracles do happen! There's nothing more important than being involved with helping people accept themselves unconditionally, gain self-respect, and break that generational cycle of low self-esteem.

YOU NEVER CAN TELL

You never can tell when you send a word
Like an arrow shot from a bow
By an archer blind, be it cruel or kind,
Just where it may chance to go.
It may pierce the breast of your dearest friend,
Tipped with its poison or balm,
To a stranger's heart in life's great mart
It may carry its pain or its calm.

You never can tell when you do an act
Just what the result will be,
But with every deed you are sowing a seed,
Though the harvest you may not see.
Each kindly act is an acorn dropped
In God's productive soil;
You may not know, but the tree shall grow
With shelter for those who toil.

You never can tell what your thoughts will do
In bringing you hate or love,
For thoughts are things, and their airy wings
Are swifter than carrier doves.
They follow the law of the universe—
Each thing will create its kind,
And they speed o'er the track to bring you back
Whatever went out from your mind.
Ella Wheeler Wilcox

RELEASING BARRIERS

Affirmations don't always come easy—especially when we have a sharp, biting reply on the tip of our tongue! However, we need to realize that when we don't respond in a non-affirming way we don't give in. Critical people set themselves up for more pain. Somewhere in their background, they have confused argumentativeness, criticism, and negativity with love. By choosing not to play this game, we are saying, "This game hurts too much. It doesn't benefit anyone and it creates more pain."

You absolutely have the power to decide which direction you want to go. This is empowering! You can have everything else in the world, yet if you don't have the ability to love people, you don't have anything. You can have fancy persuasive closes and other ways to deal with people, If you don't have love, none of it will work in the long run.

Being honest and really caring for people—*and* doing it over a period of time so that they know you're serious about it—has worked from the beginning of time.

On occasion, we get drawn into these unhealthy patterns. However, if we focus, discipline ourselves, organize our thoughts, keep our priorities straight, and make sure we're on a planned approach for desired outcomes, we can render these previous patterns harmless.

RELEASING FEAR

We are all taught from the time we are little children that the best way to cope with fear is to face it head on. The acrostic of FEAR is *False—Evidence—Appearing—Real.*

Stop dealing with fear and start taking action. Face the fear and it will reveal itself in its true size and form. If I have a fear of something, I will consciously adjust the offending thoughts. It's a process that doesn't happen automatically. If we don't make adjustments, we are not using common sense. We're not trusting the truth of what we know.

Fear doesn't have to hook you. You can let go of the fear.

Worry is a favorite companion of fear. It's inaccurate goal-setting reminding yourself of what you *don't* want to happen. Denis Waitley says, "You always move in the direction of your dominant thought." Therefore, if you're moving toward your dominant thought, and your mind is on what you don't want to happen, you're moving toward what you *don't* want to happen.

Have you ever found "that which you've feared the most has come upon you"? Have you ever been driving down the road and you look off at something, maybe a car that's off on the shoulder, and you look up and your car had swerved right over where you were looking? You look to the other side and you swerve back over in the other lane. We always seem to go to the place where we're focused.

Get a thick pad of paper and write down everything you can worry about in order of priority. Now worry about everything you have on the list. Take eight solid hours, worry as hard as you can. The next morning write a list of all of the benefits of your concentrated worry time. You might have a headache or a nervous stomach. The bottom line is worrying does not solve or change anything.

When we see the polarity in the way things work, we save ourselves a lot of time, pain, and wasted "mental gymnastics". So, my suggestion? List your worries, list the benefits, and then decide how valuable it is for you to worry! Sometimes, we simply need to let it be. Then focus our energy on what we are after, no longer focusing on what we are not after.

Ninety-two percent of the things we worry about *are in the past. And we can't do anything about those things.*

Now of the other 8%, 4% are in the future and are determined by what we do now. We can't do anything about the future, We can do something about the present. So focus on what you can do. The other 4%, are things imposed on us from the outside that we cannot control. We do have a choice to accept or resist. If we resist it, it eats up energy. If we accept it, we get on with our life.

St. Francis of Assisi wisely prayed,

"God grant me the wisdom to accept the things I cannot change; to change the things I can; and the wisdom to know the difference."

Memorize that serenity prayer, hold it in the forefront of your mind, and make sure that you practice saying it. Then let go of the need to control everything.

GENERAL MANAGER OF THE UNIVERSE

I have my life to live and

I am learning as I go

I don't know it all yet and

Still the fact is this is what I know

There is something in me I want to get out
Whether it is by poetry or by song
It won't be silenced any more
By voices from the maddening throng.

What's done is done I'm moving on,
I think I'm free at last
Free from the guilt, free from the pain
Of never living up in the past

Just let go is my new refrain
I say it again and again and again
And again and again and again and again
And again and again

I just quit trying to figure it out
I'm not smart enough for that my friend
To think I could for the longest time
Was one of my greatest sins

All I know is that when I run things
It seems to end up in a mess.
All of my fancy knowledge seems
To get in the way I confess.

I guess I forgot about what I had learned
From Adam and Eve and the fall
Being the General Manager of the Universe
Is the biggest job of all.

I now know I'm not up to that
It was never delegated to me
I just regret it has taken so much
of my life to finally see

That's not my job so I fired myself

And have been thankful ever since.

No need to be in charge or in control

Or even come to my own defense

So like naive children in paradise

We may still have a lot go wrong

We live our life the best we can

Until the next life lesson comes along

We learn our lessons bit by bit

By personal struggle they are won

When we look back at our enemies fought

To our surprise, we were the only one.

Bill Cantrell

RELEASING JUDGMENTAL ATTITUDES

When you hear these words, how does it make you feel? "Do you know what you *should* do? You *should. . .*"

Most of the time when somebody tells us what we *should, ought, or must* do, we don't want to do it. We feel they couldn't possibly understand everything involved! If anybody's going to be critical, we'll be critical of ourselves!

What if our languaging was non-judgmental? Giving people permission to make their own decisions about their life. You educate people, hoping to help them make more appropriate choices. Ultimately, you want to leave the final decision to them. Anything you do for someone you care about that they could have obviously done for themselves impacts their self-esteem. For example, when you blurt out an answer that they could have figured out for themselves had you been silent for a moment longer, that robs the individual of self-discovery.

If we aren't careful we create a dependency relationship that is not respectful of the other persons capability. When someone asks us for advice, if we aren't careful we'll jump in and try to "fix" the situation by "telling" and "judging." What if we instead ask and listen to them about what kind of outcome they want? Then ask what they believe they can do to make it possible. For example, "What are your alternatives and which one would work the best?" Help them discover their own answer.

RELEASING RESISTANCE

Have you ever been in a situation where things did not turn out the way you planned? In 1978, I was in Bloomington, Minnesota. There was a knock at the door of the apartment we rented to promote a huge Positive Thinking Rally—there were 17,000 people coming in for this rally. I opened the door and there were two men in overcoats that said they needed to speak with Mr. Bill Cantrell.

When I said I was Bill Cantrell, they asked me to please step outside. When I was outside they said, "Mr. Cantrell, you're under arrest."

"What do you mean, under arrest? Is this some sort of a joke or something?"

The one man said, "No, sir, and you need to come with us down to the police station."

"Wait a minute," I replied, "What would you want to arrest me for?"

"Somebody has accused you of armed robbery, in the Sheraton parking lot. They described your vehicle, said the assailant was less than 6 feet tall, had brown hair, brown eyes, a mustache, and spoke with a southern accent. Mr. Cantrell, how many people do you think that description fits in Bloomington, Minnesota?"

"Well, I know we'll figure this whole thing out, but I'm getting the feeling y'all are serious about this."

They said, "Mr. Cantrell, conviction of this crime carries a 30-year sentence. There's no joking about it." So they "escorted" me down to the Bloomington, MN police department. They took my tie and my belt (so I wouldn't hang myself) and the shoestrings out of my shoes. Then they took a couple of pictures of me and locked me by myself in a cell.

I was actually pleased they were taking my picture because I knew if they had my accuser try and pick me out of a stack of photos, there was no way she'd pick my picture out. I didn't do it—I wasn't even at the Sheraton—and there's *no way* she could know me. About 40 minutes later one of the officers, Lt. Whitehead, leaned on the bars and said, "Mr. Cantrell, I don't know how to tell you this. She picked your picture out three times in a row."

I was shocked, to say the least. I was sitting in this jail cell trying to figure out what to do. I don't know if you've ever been in a situation like this (hopefully not!). My mind started playing all kinds of tricks. I started thinking, what if they keep making mistakes and what if I ended up staying in here for a while? That can happen—and there have to be innocent people in jail right now. I know it could happen to me—and it could happen to someone you know—or even you.

Then I started thinking about old gangster movies and my mind started racing! So I got up and went to the cell door and asked, "Could you get me something to read? My mind's really playing tricks on me and I'd rather have something to read to keep my mind occupied."

Lt. Whitehead replied, "Well, sometimes they keep a Gideon Bible in there, I don't know—they don't last too long—I'll see what I can find." He came back and he had this book—it was swollen with the ruffled pages of water damage. Well, I looked around in the jail cell and there was only one place I could see that it could have gotten that wet!

Still, I sat down and I opened the old, ruffled Gideon Bible to a verse in Philippians. I thought if there was ever a time to read about joy, it would probably be now. I knew what it said, and I didn't really want to read it, however I did. It said, "Rejoice, again I say, rejoice in *all* things."

And I thought, "*Now?* I'm supposed to rejoice, *now?*" I kept on reading. It went on to say, "Offer everything up in prayer" and "Have peace that passes all understanding." I thought, "Boy, if there was ever a time to pray, and if there was ever a time I needed some peace about things turning out OK, now is the time." My mind kept saying, "What if you end up staying in here?" Because it *is* possible. I kept reading and got to this verse "Think on these things: Whatsoever things are right...just...pure...positive...of good report...if there be any virtue or praise, think on these things."

I thought, "I've been wearing myself out, fighting the fact that I'm here and it's not helping me or changing anything." So, I chose not to resist where I was. I let it go.

You won't believe what happened. I was sitting in the jail cell praying, "OK, Lord, if something happens and I end up staying longer than I plan, then I'll just do my work here. Maybe I could teach a class inside the jailhouse, or whatever." I didn't know what I'd do, so I decided I'd do the best I could.

As soon as I came to this conclusion, I was reminded of the Apostle Paul. Paul actually wrote these words to the Philippians from jail—he was on death row encouraging others. The thought inspired me. I'd love to have the ability, regardless of the circumstance, to be able to release it and feel certain something beneficial would come of it.

What happened next, you may find hard to believe however it's absolutely true. Lt. Whitehead came up to the jail cell and he leaned against the bars. He was a bit awkward. "You know, Cantrell, I'd like to ask you a question or two about relationships. It seems you know a lot about these things. . ."

We talked for a while about self-esteem, feelings and other topics. Finally, he said, "Something I want to ask you, and I don't know how to say this, my wife and I haven't been getting along very well." Then, after a pause, he said, "I am afraid she is going to leave me. I was wondering if you might have any suggestions because I don't know what to do." I was amazed. Here I was sitting inside the jail cell and Lt. Whitehead was outside. Yet, I was "free" and he was the one in "prison" with his relationship issues. Even though I was single at the time, I could feel the gut-wrenching pain he was going through. I suggested he go to a bookstore and pick up a copy of *Counseling*, a great book with information on working through personal and marital problems.

After we finished the conversation, it occurred to me that I never would have felt comfortable talking had I kept up the battle in my head. In fact, I could have said, "Hey, listen. You've got me here against my will—I didn't do anything. I may have to be in here, I don't have to talk to you."

Because we talked, I saw results the next morning. Lt. Whitehead came to release me. He said, "Mr. Cantrell, we tried to get this girl in here to make a positive ID and she chose not to come. Her mother got on the phone and said they wanted to drop the whole thing because there had been a big mix-up." I wanted to know what kind of mix-up!

As it turned out, this girl had been involved in some kind of cult group and the parents had recently rescued her and "kidnapped" her out of the cult. The girl was obviously going through some intense psychological adjustments. Her mother wondered if she might have made this whole situation up just to get attention!

I said, "Can I go now? When can I get out of here?" He said what I longed to hear, "You're free to go." As I was leaving, Lt. Whitehead said, "You know what? I went and got that book. It was really strange, in the first chapter it said, if you're going to fight or argue with your spouse, make sure you fight long enough." He continued, "That's exactly what I needed to hear. My wife and I would argue every morning before I left for work. We'd argue and then we'd just leave and go to work, never reaching a conclusion. The whole day we'd have this churning inside of us and we'd be just miserable. We'd come back home, continue the argument, go to bed arguing, wake up and start a new one. It never ended. I've come to the conclusion that when we argue in the future, I'm going to make sure we finish before we go to work."

He ended by saying, "I don't know whether or not this is going to help, I'm going to work on this and see what happens. I'm going to talk about this with my wife when I get home." He told me that "of all the people I've had in this facility, that your the only one that I could honestly say I was glad you were here." I was tempted to say thank you I really enjoyed my stay, yet it didn't seem appropriate. Did that man's marriage benefit from our conversation and my book referral? I believe it's possible. It's also possible I could have resisted and missed an opportunity to be of service—which is what I want to be about. Was it pleasant? Absolutely not.

When I got out of that Bloomington jail cell, I had a two-day old beard and all I'd eaten was a cold hamburger. I was hungry, my clothes were wrinkled, and I felt pretty miserable. In fact, when a friend came to pick me up, he took one look at me and joked that I even looked like a criminal! "Well, thanks," I said, "I appreciate that!"

When I walked outside, the air did smell cleaner, the food tasted better, and the sunshine felt warmer and brighter than ever before. I was more appreciative of my freedom. This was a significant emotional event in my life. It was a critical incident and a turning point for me. I wouldn't have missed it for the world. Of course, the outcome could have been different. One of the more unthinkable things could have happened. I could have been incarcerated—maybe even serving a thirty year sentence. I believe that could was possible. It did not turn out that way and I learned so much from the experience.

I'd encourage you, if there's an issue you're dealing with that you have questions about or maybe you're wondering what purpose it has in your life, let it go, stop resisting, and see what value you can get out of it.

Don't miss the value. It is in there somewhere. You may not know it yet, but you're emerging on the other side. Looking back, there's tremendous wisdom, knowledge, insight, and opportunity for growth through it all. Like this situation was for me, there was a nugget of gold hidden in all the rock. I'd encourage you to stop resisting and begin looking for whatever benefit is possible in your circumstances.

FOOD FOR THOUGHT

- What reoccurring patterns can you identify in your life that could make it difficult for you to find your direction?

- Would you be willing to address those unresolved issues as a part of your ongoing preparation for growth? If so, How?

- Who in you life could you forgive including yourself to finally surrender to what is possible for your future? When will you forgive them?

- What would need to exist for you to release all of the barriers preventing you from having the life you really want?

- Are you ready to move ahead, change, grow and live in keeping with your highest ideals without fear, worry, self-criticism or getting stuck? If so, where could you begin?

CHAPTER 6

Fruit

VISION AND DREAMS

"Don't pity the blind man who cannot see; pity the sighted man who has no vision."

—paraphrase from Helen Keller

In Bill McGrane's book, *Brighten Your Day With Self-Esteem*, he asks, "Do you have dreams? What are some of the dreams you have of your life? Do you dream of better health? More money? A fulfilling career? A bigger house in an ideal location? A luxury or sports car? The latest fashion clothing? More friends? Global travel? A dignified self-sufficient retirement? Financial independence? More meaningful relationships? More time for yourself and family? What about peace of mind, a loving family, or a deep spiritual system? Just what do you dream about? Do you dream about your influence to create a world at peace? Is having more personal power important to you? Does acquiring in-depth knowledge so you can make a greater impact on the world interest you? Do you dream of taking better charge of your life? Would you like to be helping people be the best they can be? As you dream about your future lifestyle, are you willing to tell your friends about your dreams? If so, are you ready for the consequences?"

When you tell your dreams to others, do you fear ridicule, criticism and possible abandonment? Have you ever been excited about your future and then someone said, "Who do you think you are? You'll never be able to do that. So-and-so tried that and failed," or, "You always start something and never finish," or, "I like you just the way you are, don't change, What are you trying to prove." These comments are telling you to "Stay in your box, because I know you'll never accomplish your dreams." Do you allow people to destroy your dreams? I call that dream-stealing behavior. When you hear these statements, how do you feel? Are you able to sustain your energy and interest level?

Decide now, right now, to write down your dreams. Read them aloud at least three times a day. Tell your dreams only to a mentor, coach, or someone who's committed to helping you refine your choices and move toward your desired outcomes. Focus on doing whatever it takes, without harming yourself or other people, to move in the direction of your dream. To do this you may need to:

- read books

- listen to audio cassettes

- attend seminars

- ask for help

- acquire the skills you need

- find the teachers and mentors who will encourage you and not shame or embarrass you

- invest in building a powerful vocabulary so you can communicate with anyone

- start a support group of four people who are willing to travel with you on your journey to success

- write your dreams down in a journal

Just as exercise and proper nutrition build a strong, flexible body, daily investment in your competence moves you toward the realization of your dreams.

The Japanese have a term, 'kaisan', meaning, 'incremental growth'. They also have five hundred-year business and personal plans. They have an understanding of how one layer at a time can eventually accomplish the goal. You and I can follow their example by investing incrementally to realize our long-range goals.

Richard Bach, most famous for his *Jonathan Livingston Seagull* book, said, "Here's a test to find whether your mission on earth is finished. If you're alive, it isn't." If we're here, there's got to be something we can do. If we don't know what our mission is and don't find out, then we're going to miss out on the sense of desire and focused direction it would provide. Do you have a dream you would like to move toward as time goes by? Wouldn't you like your business to facilitate your dream? Desired success, in business, can allow you to accomplish your dreams. Yet, what happens to your vision of the dream if your business isn't working the way you had planned? Your dream moves further away. Along with it goes your belief in what you can accomplish in your business.

Keeping an awareness of your mission and vision in your work helps keep your compelling motivation in focus. It is also a way to begin clarifying what we're really after. I believe all the realities and events that go on around us are not realities, but distractions from our reality. We are sidetracked into thinking the overwhelming daily tasks are what we need to focus upon. Then we lose the glimpse of our dream that we experienced. We only get glimpses of our dream. If we don't hold onto it and make it a reality, it dies for lack of nurturing, falling prey to our internal doubts.

SCULPTURE BOY

Chisel in hand stood a sculpture boy,

his marble block before him,

And his eyes lit up with a smile of joy

as an angel dream passed o'er him.

He carved it then, in the shapeless stone,

with many a sharp incision

And with Heaven's own light that sculpture shone

he'd caught the angel vision.

Children of life are we as we stand,

our life uncarved before us,

Awaiting the hour when at Heaven's command,

our life dream shall pass o'er us.

If we carve it then in the yielding stone

with many a sharp incision

With Heaven's own beauty that sculpture will show

we've become our angel vision.

Unknown

GETTING OUR MISSION CLEAR

If we don't work for our dream, we miss out on what was possible. It's not about just trying to make money, or having material possessions. It's about being honest with ourselves, who we are, what we stand for, represent, believe in, and what we're really about. If we have integrity, I think we can begin to find our way back to our mission. Even if it is difficult and challenging, we'll know we are moving in the right direction. I don't think convenience is really what we're after. Comfort doesn't satisfy us like being on target in our life. That's what we're truly interested in, but sometimes we forget and settle for things like temporary pleasure or comfort, taking time off, hiding out, or giving in. However, we know it won't last, and it begins to bother us after a while.

This is something that runs deeper than winning a prize, or going for the next level. Those things are important, but if you are after something greater than yourself you will have more strength, energy, and desire to push ahead. The mere accomplishment of a goal, if it is not of your larger dream, is not as powerful a reward. Our goals are a smaller component of motivation and planning. Goals are subservient to our mission, purpose, and our outcomes.

Goals have not always worked for me. Many times goals were de-motivating rather than motivating, whether I wanted them to be or not. If you reach a goal, immediately you're expected make a bigger one, and to continue on. Consequently, there is very little satisfaction in reaching the goals you've set. Hard work for goal accomplishment is not a fair trade because it is never enough.

GOALS AND OUTCOMES

There's a difference between a goal and an outcome. A goal is something you either make or you don't; it's unyielding. There isn't any flexibility in the accomplishment of a goal. We can choose not to reach the goal, or we can choose to change the goal along the way when we see we're not going to meet the deadline yet the goal does not change. Sometimes we do not pull away and look at the larger picture of our life to see if we're really headed in the direction we would like to go. This is a great time to take a look at where you're headed to see if your goals match your desired outcomes.

Outcomes are designed to provide a governing parameter so that the goals we set, and the objectives that we have, fit within our mission. Our outcomes will govern our objectives and our goals. Our outcomes are flexible. They are not limited by time. Instead, outcomes are things we can maintain even if it's not the ideal. We can continue to refine it, change, polish, and buff, in order to eventually have an ideal outcome.

As long as we refine and work at our art, craft, or business, eventually the desired outcomes are going to materialize. Our goals and objectives fit within our mission to move us toward the desired outcomes, so that when we set a goal we know it can afford to be unyielding. It might be for some of the smaller, more controllable areas of our life. If we set goals that are going to be determined by the compliance of another person, we could be setting ourselves up for failure. We need some control over our goals and our objectives. Don Hutson once said that "there are no unrealistic goals, just unrealistic time frames".

Many times we can accomplish what we set out to do, yet we set unrealistic time parameters or objectives that don't give us the flexibility we need. There could be pressing issues that demand our attention, consequently making the objectives impossible to meet. Likewise, we do not give ourselves the time we need to cope with transition or a life crisis.

Goals and objectives play an important role because we have certain things we need to get done to meet the criteria other people give us for incentive, or to be the best in what we do and to achieve the levels of recognition we desire. We need to meet the criteria with goals and objectives. However, when we have more flexibility, we know that time is something we use to create a picture that falls in line with our vision, mission, and purpose. We want to refine, continue to grow, change as needed so that what we are doing works for us and produce the outcomes we want. If we have our vision, mission, and purpose, as well as our desired outcomes defined, we can know how to use short-term time effectively.

BUSINESS PLAN FLOW CHART

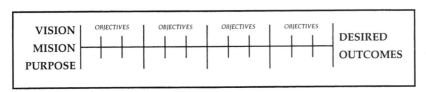

The Business Plan Flow Chart is divided into four quarters with, of course, three months in each quarter. I'd like you to begin to think about specific objectives for month one, month two, and month three. Take some of the practical information we've already evaluated (or things that could be preventing you from getting the results you want) and put them into your plan so you can do something about them in the first quarter. You can use this chart from one year to the next. When you're ready to do some planning for part of your year or for the year as a whole, pull your Business Plan Flow Chart out and ask yourself,

- Where am I on my way to accomplishing my life mission?

- Do I still have the same purpose?

- What is my vision for one year from now, or for the time period I would like to plan?

- Are there still specific desired outcomes I'd like to accomplish along the way?

- What are the goals and objectives that will create the outcomes I'm after within my mission.

I've found this is a simple system to make sure our personal, strategic planning is complete. If we are clear on our personal mission, we have a context for the outcomes we'd like to produce. Our fruit is what comes from our effort and investment in following our dream. Fruit is what we produce in the lives of other people. It's also what we see coming out of our own life.

CREATING BALANCE

Rich Meiss, a friend and consummate training professional, stated that success could be defined as having enough in every area of our life. The areas of our life are: Spiritual, Mental, Emotional, Physical, Social, Financial, Career and Family. If we have one area of our life that requires more of our time and attention than others, then we could be deficient in more than one other area of our life. For instance, if our career becomes the primary focus of our time and attention, then what happens to our personal life? Could we disqualify ourselves from moving ahead and fulfilling the dream by failing to accept that we have more than one area of life and we're responsible to each one of them? If we are going to be healthy and fruitful in every area, we need to change our priorities to be in keeping with our overall mission and desired outcome.

TWO BIRDS FIGHTING

Sitting outside I watched two birds fighting today

My baby played just a few steps away

Reminded how just a few months ago she had learned to walk

Mentally, I imagined her words as if she could talk.

This was the first time this year my thoughts were clear.

I regret to report it's taken half the year to get here.

Being out of balance is now a common place thing.

Our current lifestyles demand devotion to multiple things.

Our parents were faced with different life choices

They made it through by listening to their inner voices

Our choices also tell us what we value best

Learning who we are and what we want,

our most challenging test.

I watched two birds fighting today

My baby played just a few feet away

I wondered to myself was I missing the mark

Do I build a bigger business or have a picnic at the park?

When faced with such a decision before

Business opportunity came knocking at my door.

As soon as I scheduled full my business day

My mind would immediately turn to family and play.

When I desired personal time to have an ideal family life.

Lack of choices and money created internal strife.

I watched two birds fighting today.

I watch my baby play just a few feet away.

I knew the consequence of ignoring my economic needs

An inner voice questioned, are you living beyond your means?

I wrestled with the conflict of wasted time spent.

When that same time could be invested to pay the rent.

When people with great persuasion invited me to go

I asked was this producing what I wanted or do I say no.

Some I see want to be balanced in the time span of a day,

Others say to be balanced in a month or a year would be O.K.

The secret is clarifying what you want for you and all

Then disciplining yourself to heed that inner personal call.

I watched two birds fighting today.

My baby played just a few feet away.

Bill Cantrell

DISCIPLINING OUR THOUGHT LIFE TOWARD BALANCE

What if we learned to talk to ourselves in a healthy way? Would it make a difference in the development of our undeveloped areas. The following guidelines are a suggested format for refining out thoughts to better insure they are in alignment with our vision and mission.

FIVE GUIDELINES

1. **Personal**. Begin sentences with "I am." Use first-person words.

2. **Positive**. Describe attitudes and feelings you want to acquire and maintain.

3. **Present**. Focus on the *now*. Use *present moment* statements like, "I now live my life in such a way that the future I envision is a reality."

4. **Produced**. Express the result as already produced.

5. **Performance**. Avoid comparisons; describe your activity rather than ability.

Have you ever heard anybody say that when you want to pray or affirm something, do so as if it's already happened? I have experienced the power of disciplined and undisciplined thinking, and prayer. At the beginning of my road career, I was working on a sales seminar with Zig Ziglar and other top speakers. I found myself in Virginia's tidewater area. I had been making 30 cold calls a day for a couple of weeks when my car started acting up. Fear entered my mind. This program was critical for survival in my dream career. If this program was not financially successful, my options would be severely limited. It was time to fish or cut bait. If I made it financially on this program, I could continue in my chosen career. If not....

My prayer sounded something like this: "Lord, help my car. I need this car to make it to the end of the program. I need this program to be successful. Please help my car keep running until the program is over."

When my car hung in there for the next few weeks, I chalked it up to powerful prayer, disciplined thinking and a guardian angel.

After the program, when I walked to the car and turned the key, it was completely dead. Not even a click. It cost me close to $300 to repair the car enough to make it back home and retire it from service. Then I bought a new car with the money I made at the program. This experience is a constant reminder to me that thoughts and prayers are powerful. Be careful what you think about all day. If I had prayed that the car make it all the way home, I could have saved that $300. My new prayer might sound like this, "Lord, thank you in advance for getting me through the program and back home safely in my car."

THE MYSTERY OF THE BRAIN

I'm fascinated by the workings of the brain. I've spent hours talking to neurosurgeons and psychiatric experts. The "reticular activating system", a network of cells at the base of the brain, automatically continues to support the idea (or seed) you plant. When you plant a thought, the reticular activating system begins to work. It won't allow a replacement contrary to the thought you're committed to.

Let's use an example from real life. I think it might help to illustrate this principle. A neighbor told me he discovered something strange. He had just bought a new car, a white GMC Suburban. Suddenly he realized there were white GMC Suburbans *everywhere*, just like his. Now it's probably not likely that the Suburban dealer had a huge sale and everyone in the area bought cars just like my neighbor's on the same weekend! The cars like his were already there. He just hadn't noticed until he bought his!

The same type of occurrence recently happened when a friend of mine had to attend a fund raising banquet. She decided to wear a recently purchased dress and was mortified when she saw her new dress on two other women! The other women had the dress in different colors—it was the same exact dress, nonetheless! My guess is that she would not have noticed that particular dress on the two other women if she hadn't bought it for herself.

You plant the seed in your reticular activating system and begin to be aware of details that might have passed by you before. What if you planted seeds for bookings or recruits? What if you planted seeds of beliefs and taking action for more business?

Ultimately, you can't fool yourself. Just do your part and plant the affirming thought to give yourself a chance. Then reinforce them enough so that they can make a difference toward the ideal balanced life outcomes that you are after. Repetition is the first step to implanting these disciplined thoughts.

BALANCED LIFE AFFIRMATIONS

SPIRITUAL

1. ..."Whatsoever things are true, whatsoever things are honest, whatsoever things are just, whatsoever things are pure, whatsoever things are love-

ly, whatsoever things are of good report; if there be any virtue, if there be any praise, think on these things." Philippians. 4:8.

This is one life verse that has personal significance. If you don't have these kinds of strong emotional and spiritually based affirmations for your life, what will you do when you need support and encouragement? My suggestion is that you focus on reinforcing this area of your life. There are other areas of your life you can influence as well. I intentionally put spiritual first because, to me, the spiritual aspect of your life is a filter that influences other things. No other area will make the contribution you need when you're dealing with difficult issues.

2. "In all my ways I now acknowledge Him, and I know He will continue to direct my paths." Proverbs 3:6.

FINANCIAL

Affirmations will not automatically make you a financial genius if you're having financial problems. You can study and use your intellectual gifts to increase your abundance.

1. "I am prosperity. Prosperity is the law of my life. My supply is wherever I am. I feel this abundance coming to me from every direction. I accept this unlimited flow of well-being. I know everyone I meet will benefit from this prosperity now."

Have you ever felt money was an issue—managing, making more, or making particular amounts of money? I heard a story about a salesperson who worked one large territory in his company. He earned about $5,000 a year (this was back a number of years ago when that was a significant sum of money for a salesperson!). The next year, because he had done such a fantastic job, they gave him the best territory in the company. He piddled around and didn't live up to his potential or the company's expectations. He earned $5,000 again. Instead of firing him, they put him in the smallest territory. So the next year he worked harder than he'd ever worked before and still made $5,000. It sounds like he set a ceiling on his earning potential!

Do you think that if you and I set some kind of arbitrary cap or ceiling on how much money you could make, it would be enough? It could be. Can you do your work? Can you get your message out? Can you make a contribution to others? Do you need more? Is your mind so tied up with financial issues that you can't focus on building a business? If it is, then release financial stress out of your life. You don't need it. It's a source of tension. It will tie you up into a stressful knot.

I got to the point where I was tired of living that way. If you've had enough, you don't settle for that kind of lifestyle anymore. Instead, you change things. I changed things. Still, I am constantly working on every one of these areas. It is satisfying to see progress in every area.

2. "I am receiving a never-ending, ever-increasing supply of money into my life. I deserve it, will use it for my good and that of others." Now, do we have any guarantee that will happen? No. Chances are, if we affirm it in advance we're going to be attracted to that level of business. *Affirm it in advance.*

If you're saying, "I'm going to have an every-increasing supply of money", and then inside, you say, "yeah, it'll probably be an ever-decreasing supply of money," well you can bet that affirmation won't have any power. It only is as powerful as the strength of the belief behind it. If you don't believe it, then it does not have any power. The affirmation cannot change things without belief. It won't make a difference unless you really believe it and do it.

MENTAL

1. I am now reading books, listening to tapes, participating in positive, reinforcing workshops, programs, and classes. I have a constant influx of new information crossing my thoughts daily, expanding my awareness of myself, other people and the world around me.

2. My mind is constantly creating new ideas to help me accomplish my mission in life. I am now developing my mind in a systematic way, to serve my personal development, my family and my business daily.

SOCIAL

1. I am now building a large network of friends and customers who are attracted to me. My giving spirit and non-judgmental ways permit me to naturally make new friends. I am genuinely interested in helping others meet their needs and feel supported now.

2. I am now building loving trust relationships that permit disclosure and honesty. I unconditionally accept myself and others just the way they are now. My actions are consistently in alignment with my promises."

PHYSICAL

A friend from Jackson, Mississippi, told me he lost thirty-two pounds by thinking thin. It wasn't that easy, because he started thinking in a definite direction he began craving different kinds of food. When he started craving different kinds of food, he also changed his activities. It was a step-by-step process to get to the healthy framework he desired.

1. Instead of worrying about gaining weight, think about thinness, health, and lifestyle. Affirm with yourself: "I am getting thinner. Everything I eat converts to energy that I use to accomplish great things for my own business."

2. I am increasing my stamina, energy and vitality daily. I eat foods that are healthy for my body, mind and spirit. I look great, feel great and am making wise choices for my physical health now.

CAREER

1. I am now living my dream of having a business that generates income to meet my needs, and makes a meaningful difference in my life and that of others.

2. I am now developing the skills, abilities, business contacts and the willingness to take action in order to generate outstanding ongoing business results, while meeting my lifestyle needs in every major area of my life—including spiritual, financial, mental, social, physical and career.

This is the affirmation process. Changing our lifestyle to have our life healthy is a self-esteem issue for all of us. Just how much do you believe you deserve to live a different life than you are living now? Success takes focus and work. Review your spiritual, financial, mental, social physical and career relationships and make sure they **create** a supportive atmosphere so that you can find your direction!

These affirmations are such healthy thoughts to hold in our minds. My personal preference is Scripture and poetry. I love poems with profound messages that apply to me. You might have songs that mean a great deal to you. I have a song I sing in the shower every day. When the water hits my back, that's the anchor for me to start singing. I feel great after I sing. Create your own affirmations. Sometimes the beginning of change is a simple adjustment. Think about health, or lifestyle. Think toward things you want to become. You will move in the direction you are looking. You now have a practical way to immediately begin to move towards *reinforcing your direction*.

FOOD FOR THOUGHT

- What have you always dreamed of becoming?

- How do you envision the ideal life and lifestyle for your family?

- Can you give yourself permission to receive that level of satisfaction and joy? How can you reinforce that concept daily?

- When you have enough in every area, how could you better give yourself away in service to others?

- What lasting legacy would you like to leave that would live long after you are gone?

CHAPTER 7

Harvest

If we look over our history, we see significant emotional events, turning points, and life experiences that have shaped our direction. When we make a commitment to accomplish our life direction, we identify and leave behind barriers that stand in the way. Fruit (spiritual, mental, emotional, physical, and financial) is the natural outcome for our lives as we follow our direction. When we define our direction, we identify our philosophy of life, our purpose in pursuing our mission, and we clarify our values and beliefs. Our life function then becomes an avocation—an adjunct to our vocational mission.

We need to give it the energy it requires so that we stay healthy and continue to become even healthier. Begin to max out your creativity. Don't sacrifice one area of your life for the over-fulfillment of another. So you make plenty of money. What if your mental and emotional life is dead? There are disconnected people trading off one area of their life for another, taking the consequences, all the time.

If you accept responsibility for taking these things into consideration and make a decision about what's next in your life, the results could prove to be much better than before. If you take into consideration who you are, where you come from, and the patterns you may be repeating, you can make positive choices in finding your direction. You can leave destructive patterns behind to begin doing what you may have been fearful of doing before. I have used my story as an example of how we can take responsibility for our life's direction. Realizing our dreams is not easy, we can take action by dealing with our past. We deal with our past so that we can use our present to shape our future. If we want to accomplish our dreams, we do not allow others to shape our direction for us and we begin to stretch and grow more personally .

We take a great chance relying only on our senses and determining our direction on our own, especially when it's based on temporary circumstances or our immediate needs. I now know and believe there's a better way to determine what to do next with our lives. Through a deep and abiding faith in God early in life, a reliance on the gentle direction of God through people, and life events, my life direction has become more obvious to me. A reliance on those guideposts and benchmarks have taught me to trust even when the next step is not so obvious. Reading clues and learning to recognize them when they appear is the very essence of life, in that we are learning to trust God with our future.

The mighty oak grows from a tiny acorn seed into a strong tree that is able to face the changing seasons. Like us, the tree encounters many environmental factors that hinder its ability to reach its full potential. Yet, unlike the tree, we are able to take responsibility for our lives so that we can work through barriers that hinder our growth. We reach our potential by defining our issues, addressing them, and consequently, we develop our own story. The environment where we were born (healthy or unhealthy) can only temporarily determine our focus. As long as we accept personal responsibility for the lessons of our life, we can recover in time from almost any life event.

Allowing others to help guide, direct, and support us is not always easy if people have let us down in the past. However, with faith in God's love and the ability to gradually forgive ourselves and others, we can develop a whole new identity that allows us to be who we are created to be. We can let go of our old identity which many times is based on distorted information. When we know who we are, and begin to honor our preparation through life experiences, we can branch off and begin our best work. This allows us to make a valid contribution to the world that no one else can give.

If we begin our life's work with a degree of personal integrity, we can allow the setbacks to come and go. We can stay focused on doing what we are here to accomplish. No one can take our place or make our contribution to the world. We have such a wonderful gift to give, like a precious one-of-a-kind heirloom that can be a legacy for others' benefit long after we are gone. If we really commit to living a full life, then we may become aware of our need to leave our old patterns behind. Anything that may hold us back is our responsibility to address out of our commitment to our life's work.

When we are challenged by these life events, we can look back and realize we were simply being tested to see if we could be persuaded to cave in or give up. When we stand fast, the old identity crumbles and we emerge on the other side. We become a new person, ready to move on and produce great outcomes in every area of our lives, to be fruitful, receiving all of the great gifts that I believe God holds for us until we are ready. Life becomes full of possibilities and we are no longer fighting so hard with ourselves. By simply telling the truth, we testify as to the rich personal insight we have gained. We let others know even if it's not easy living this way it's worth it.

We now can be who we are, thankful to have learned our life lessons so that we can teach others. This is a process of evaluating our "*seeds*" *of heredity* that are wired in. Then acknowledge that our *early environmental "roots"* taught us some patterns and beliefs we can redesign later as our knowledge, wisdom, and skills develop.

Take a look at all of the dedicated teachers and mentors that gave of themselves so we could learn how to do everything from tying our shoes, to riding our first bike, to sorting out the feeling of our first love, to finally stepping off the high ledge of our secure nest, to fly as we felt the wind in our wings for the first time. Our teachers and mentors made sure our "*trunk*" developed solidly. As we "*branch out*" on our own, we can show our appreciation for their great influence by becoming the person they saw that we could be.

Committing ourselves to our work and letting go of anything that might stand in the way lets us choose to let the "*leaves*" of old, reoccurring patterns fall from our tree. Entering into the Dream and realizing we have nothing to lose except our true selves helps us to live a life that reaches our full potential. Living at this level produces more "*fruit*" in every area of your life.

My fervent prayer is that you can take a long look at your life and reflect in prayer and meditation on your own unique story. As you reflect, allow the ideal next step in your direction making process to emerge. The next step is there waiting for you to identify it. When you begin to see, hear, feel, accept, and act on it, you will have discovered one of the great secrets of a life worth living. You will know there is rhyme and reason to everything. There is a process for finding your direction.

"In all thy ways acknowledge him, and he shall direct thy paths."
—*Proverbs 3:6*

QUOTATIONS

Commit thy way unto the Lord; trust also in him; and he
shall bring it to pass.

—Psalm 37:5

But indeed, 'tis not so much for its beauty that the forest makes a claim
upon men's hearts, as for the subtle something, that quality of air, that
emanation from the old well-developed trees that so
wonderfully changes and renews a weary spirit.
—Robert Lewis Stevenson

What was paradise? But a garden, an orchard of trees and herbs full of
pleasure, and nothing there but delights.

—William Lawson

The first instinct of the stem . . .the instinct of seeking the light, as of the
root to seek darkness–what words can speak the wonder of it.

—John Ruskin

I like trees because they seem more resigned to the way they have to live
than other things do.

—Willa Cather

He that plants trees loves others beside himself.

— Unknown

In everything you do, put God first, and he will direct you and crown
your efforts with success.

— Proverbs 3:6 TLB

Trust in the Lord with all your heart and lean not on your own
understanding.

— *Proverbs 3:5 NIV*

A handful of pine seeds will cover mountains with a green majestic
forest. I too will set my face to the wind and throw my
handful of seed on high.
—*Fiona Macleod*

Our deeds are seeds of fate, sown here on earth, but bring
forth their harvest in eternity. All I have seen teaches me to trust the
Creator for all I have not seen.
—*Ralph Waldo Emerson*

It is not pride when the beech tree refuses to copy the oak.
The only chance of any healthy life for him is to be
as full of beech tree as he can be.
—*Phillip Brooks*

If seeds in the black earth can turn into such beautiful roses,
what might not the heart of man become in its long
journey toward the stars.
—*G. K. Chesterton*

Father of us all,
The birds of the air sing your praises
And the trees reach toward you.
In my own way I join them
In proclaiming your greatness.
Amen

—*Unknown*

FINDING YOUR DIRECTION
PERSONAL SURVEY

1. What seeds have prepared you for your life direction?

2 . What seeds have created challenges for you? If not rejection, what would your issues be?

3. How can you take responsibility for working through early "seed" issues? How will that enable you to use your gifts more effectively?

4. What personal responsibility would you need to take for better using your gifts and working through your early "seed" issues?

5.   How did your environment shape you?

6.   How did you learn to respond to your early environment?

7.   What was your birth order?

8,   How did your roots prepare you for what you're doing now?

9. Does your life reflect who you are inside, or are you living a lie or wearing a mask?

10. What roots and environmental influences did you have for which you now need to accept responsibility so you can move ahead?

11. Who are the teachers and mentors who made a major difference in your life?

12. Do you currently have someone who is shaping your direction and influencing your learning? Who? How?

18.   What can you do to help yourself and others meet their basic needs?

19.   In what meaningful way can you support others emotionally, giving them total unconditional acceptance?

20.   What circumstances would need to exist for you to deepen your personal commitment to your chosen direction?

21.   What reoccurring patterns can you identify in your life that could make it difficult for you to find your direction?

22.   Would you be willing to address those unresolved issues as a part of your ongoing preparation for growth? If so, How?

23.   Who in you life could you forgive including yourself to finally surrender to what is possible for your future? When will you forgive them?

24.   What would need to exist for you to release all of the barriers preventing you from having the life you really want?

25.   Are you ready to move ahead, change, grow and live in keeping with your highest ideals without fear, worry, self-criticism or getting stuck? If so, where could you begin?

26. What have you always dreamed of becoming?

27. How do you envision the ideal life and lifestyle for your family?

28. Can you give yourself permission to receive that level of satisfaction and joy? How can you reinforce that concept daily?

29. When you have enough in every area, how could you better give yourself away in service to others?

30. What lasting legacy would you like to leave that would live long after you are gone?

CAPTURE YOUR DIRECTION

Take a quiet moment, prayerfully reflect on your responses to this survey. Ask for clear direction, listen, then capture the insights on what the next step, or next phase, of your life or career need to be.

_____

_____

_____

_____

_____

_____

_____

_____

_____

_____

_____

_____

_____

beliefs	107... living by beliefs and values 110... the E Myth	I am now living what I believe.
blame	46..... and accepting responsibility	I am accepting responsibility for everything I think, say, do and feel now.
change	130... and growth 130... stages of	I am now open to change and growth as a natural part of finding my direction.
commitment	100... keeping commitments to yourself 112... doubt after making commitment 116... commitment and internal drive 118... results of keeping commitments 132... making commitments reality	I am now keeping my commitments to myself and others. I am a person of my word.
comparison	78..... to others 81..... in developing your unique factors 102... and self-esteem 106... results of	I am now willing to discover my unique factors and develop them to the fullest.

Topical index for one-on-one coaching, performance management, and mentoring

beliefs	107... living by beliefs and values 110... the E Myth	I am now living what I believe.
blame	46.... and accepting responsibility	I am accepting responsibility for everything I think, say, do and feel now.
change	130... and growth 130... stages of	I am now open to change and growth as a natural part of finding my direction.
commitment	100... keeping commitments to yourself 112... doubt after making commitment 116... commitment and internal drive 118... results of keeping commitments 132... making commitments reality	I am now keeping my commitments to myself and others. I am a person of my word.
comparison	78.... to others 81..... in developing your unique factors 102... and self-esteem 106... results of	I am now willing to discover my unique factors and develop them to the fullest.

Keyword	Reference	Affirmation
competition	102... and self-esteem	I am now willing to become the best I can possible be, and allow others the right to be self-determined.
confidence	103... and internal conflict	I am now building a sense of confidence in my abilities as I increase my base of experience.
customers	82..... and feedback	I am now listening to my customers and refining my service according to their feedback.
creativity	22..... in sales	I am now using creativity to meet my clients needs, wants and values in the sales process.
decisions	14..... basing decisions on the merits of the situation 113... and doubt 121... life decisions	I am now looking on my life as a whole, asking for help and making decisions that are healthy and forward moving.

Term	References	Affirmation
DIRECT method	76..... explanation of	I am now accepting the challenge to grow fully and learn from every stage of my life.
direction	116... when we've found our direction 121... redirection	I am now finding my direction on a daily basis in keeping with my mission, purpose, vision and dream.
discipline	140... heart, mind and thoughts	I am now disciplining my thoughts and actions in alignment with what I believe, and the outcomes I'm after.
doubt	112... after making the commitment	I am now maintaining a singleness of purpose and focus maintained by faith and belief.
dreams	159... dream-stealing 161... focusing on	I am now asking for, clarifying and living out the Dream that God has provided me.
education	18..... as a responsibility 19..... transferring knowledge and value 21..... seeing "no's" as necessary for	I am now educating myself and others in products, services, and ideas that I believe in most.

entrepreneurs	109... and personal integrity 110... and the internal decision-making process	I am now my own person expressed through my own business.
environment	9..... and early experience 40..... impact of 43..... assuming responsibility 43..... getting unstuck 117... growth encouraging	I am now accepting responsibility for my environments, past, present and future.
family	9...... history, and how it plays a part	I am now learning and teaching the lessons I've gained from my family history.
fear	16..... in response to rejection 99..... and choosing best direction 112... as we change and grow 147... releasing fear	I am now focusing on living with love, power and a sound mind.
friends and family	115... reactions to your growth	I am now following through on my personal Dream for my own reasons.

intuition	83..... your "inner knowing" 98..... in life and work	I am now trusting my intuition and sense of knowing in addition to my own personal experience.
learning	78..... integrating new information 82..... observing as you learn 115... circles	I am now increasing my ability to learn by observing, perceiving and integrating new information.
left and right brain	47..... differences 49..... and early environment 55..... personalizing presentations 58..... utilizing both	I am now using my whole brain to produce a balanced result in my life and business.
life events	91..... lessons from	I am now learning and growing from my life events and am sharing the lessons I've learned with others.
limitations	77..... identifying	I am now developing my undeveloped skills and abilities in a systematic way in order to fulfill my chosen direction.

Category	Items	Affirmation
"no's"	17..... falling in love with 18..... questions in response to 20..... placing monetary value on	I am now providing the additional information that a "no" is asking for. Each "no" brings me closer to my desired out comes. Thanks for the twenty bucks. You can work with me now or later but sooner or later your going to work with me.
needs, wants and values	36.... determining customer needs 77..... identifying core criteria 105... the reason their important	I am now interpreting objections as an open door to share additional information. I am asking more questions so I can better identify the needs, wants and values of others. I appreciate that a lack of understanding in others allows me to provide information and hope.
negativity	112.. and friends 139... releasing negativity 140... non-affirming comments 142... protecting yourself (three-step process) 143... responding to	I am now focusing on what I want not what I don't want. I am now putting energy into the things I want to get bigger. I now believe it's better to light one candle than curse the darkness.
outcome	163... vs. goals and objectives	Each day I am doing something refines and enhances the outcome I'm after for my life and business.

over-giving	125... as unhealthy behavior	I am encouraging others to give out of their own developed areas. I am now balancing my giving with appropriate receiving to insure my desire to give.
patterns of behavior	125... growing beyond childhood behavior patterns	As an adult, I am now exercising the freedom to learn and act in a healthier way.
past	45..... and its present effect	I am utilizing my personal history to bring a clearer focus to areas of personal growth.
perfectionism	134... and procrastination	I am now willing to make mistakes because that's the way to learn. I am now doing the best I can at my current level of awareness. and the time frame I am able to invest.
persistence	14..... and fear of rejection 14..... in building value 22..... when getting "no's" 26..... and getting desired outcome	I am now staying focused on my desired outcome, and taking the action steps necessary to complete the task. I am now willing to press through challenges to find opportunities.

purpose	76..... identifying yours	I am defining my daily action plan according to the outcome I wish to achieve. I now have a clear and compelling reason to do what I am planning.
rapport	34..... questions to establish	I am seeking to understand others by listening carefully and asking questions that allow them to share about who they are and what they need.
relationships	33..... building	I am willing to invest myself into the lives of others in order to build healthy relationships now.
referral advertising	39..... example	I am providing services at such a level that others will want to educate their friends and associates about my service.
rejection	14..... affecting decision-making 14..... how it affects us 15..... avoidance behaviors and 16..... reactions to 27..... 5 steps for dealing with rejection feelings 104... and personal integrity	I now alleviate fear of rejection by building value in myself, my products, and my service while educating one layer at a time.

responsibility	91..... in growth and learning 97..... in finding direction 109... in owning own business 117... in growing our "circles"	I now choose to live my life to the fullest. I am now ready to take a big bite out of life. I am developing the ability to respond well in all situations.
roots	44..... early environmental influences 46..... root "issues"	I am now ready to accept responsibility for my personal history and life experiences.
self-discipline	110... internal accountability	I am holding myself accountable and following through with focus and discipline now.
self-esteem	75..... moving from outer driven to inner directed 97..... and approval of others 101... model for 103... and self-respect 104... self-esteem vs. self image 143... reinforcing others	I accept responsibility for keeping my self esteem intact and want to reinforce that of others now.
self-talk	29..... internal dialogue	I am now willing to affirm myself accept the affirmation of others.

self-respect	99..... in comparison with others 103... in relation to self-esteem 106... as inner directed	I am now maintaining a healthy level of self-respect by living according to what I believe. I now release any need to compare myself with others. I am now accepting responsibility for utilizing my unique factors toward fulfillment.
sharing	81..... from your own experiences 83..... and your own message 84..... and benefiting others 85..... finding your story	I am now sharing my life experiences and my message with others for their benefit.
"should, ought, and must"	74..... and value judging 105... in our thinking 151... using non-judgmental language	I am an accepting human being, totally and unconditionally accepting with out judgment.
skills	82..... refining of	I am refining my skills daily to bring me closer to my vision and mission.
superlative service	29..... example	I am an example of honesty and integrity and am known for providing superlative service.

Support Programs
Finding Your Direction Weekends

Have you ever dreamed of a place you could go to regain clarity on your life's directions? Now there is a place to do just that!

If you can envision a relaxing environment with like-minded people in an intensive direction-discovery process, then this weekend is for you. You will gain personal clarity, wisdom, and insight as you work through your own "finding your direction" process. This six-module, three-day program is designed to help you discover the next phase of your life and career. Then you will learn how to use this powerful process to impact the lives of others.

Custom-Designed Training

When you have a need for a keynote speaker, a training event, or custom designed long-term consulting intervention, let us assist you in identifying and facilitating a new direction for your organization. The topics listed below represent a partial list of programs we have designed and implemented for organizations nation-wide:

- Leadership Styles
- Term Building Building and Innovation
- Listening and the Art of Asking Questions
- Decision Making and Problem Solving
- Customized Recruiting Interviews
- Performance Management Coaching
- Building Self-Esteem in the Work Environment

- Strategic Planning
- Customer Service
- Process Selling
- Life and Time Management
- Increasing Creativity
- Needs and Values Motivation
- Communications Skills and Persuasion

Other Resources

We also suggest you consider the McGrane Institute and their in-depth high content programs including "Making It Happen!" and "Managing the Human Machine." For additional information, call **1-800-341-3304** or contact McGrane Institute at **www.mcgrane.com**.

Cantrell Training, Inc.
For a free brochure, call: **1-800-866-6903**

or contact us at: P.O. Box 6077 • Arlington, Texas 76005
Fax: (817) 277-0340
or visit our website: www.cantrelltraining.com

Resources for Continuous Growth and Development
Personal Profiles to Evaluate Your Development

Biblical Profile. (Determine which Old and New Testament Biblical Character is most like you)

Personal Profile. (4 Dimensions of Human Behavior in your natural work and relationship approach)

Relationship Profile. (For two people to work on how to support each other better while communicating)

Personal Learning Insights. (Discover how you personally prefer to learn)

Dimensions of Leadership Profile. (12 Dimensions you can use to be a more effective leader)

Time Mastery Profile. (12 Categories of Time to Master)

Personal Listening Profile. (5 Approaches to Listening, yours and the best one for others)

Coping with Stress. (4 areas of life and work to evaluate stress and your coping skills)

Values Profile. (Learn which of 4 points of view you emphasize most)

Interpersonal Profile. (How other people describe you for 360 degree feed back)

Innovate With Care Profile. (For Increasing team effectiveness)

Personal Profile Electronic Software Report. (A computer generated, in-depth evaluation of your work style)

Cassette Albums to Build and Refine Skills By Bill Cantrell

• Building Self Esteem and Your Business
• Customized Recruiting Interviews — Behavioral Styles
• Developing Leadership Skills
• Life and Time Mastery
• Listening, Questions, and Contracting
• Leadership Styles

Books

• *Finding Your Direction* (hardcover) — Quantity discounts
• *Finding Your Direction Workbook* (for small group facilitation)

The above materials are available from:
Cantrell Training, Inc. 1-800-866-6903

SUGGESTED READING LIST

Brighten Your Day With Self-Esteem. William J. McGrane, C.P.A.E. Success Publishers, 1995. (How to empower, energize, & motivate yourself to a richer, fuller, more rewarding life.)

The Creative Brain. Ned Herman Brain Book, 1995. (Brain Dominance and Creativity.)

Poems That Touch The Heart. Doubleday,1957. (Poetry that inspires.)

The Bible New International Version.

Getting Unstuck - Breaking Through Your Barriers To Change. Dr. Sidney B. Simon. Warner Books,1988. (Turn the life you have into the life you want.)

Success with People through Human Engineering & Motivation. Cavett Robert. Success Unlimited, 1969. (A simple, six step program that shows you how to attain your maximum ability to make more money and increase your personal power.)

The World of the Unborn. Dr. Leni Schwartz, Ph.D. Richard Marek Publishers, 1980. (Nurturing your child before birth.)

Influencing with Integrity. Genie Z. Laborde. Syntony Publishing, 1983, 1987. (Management skills for communication and Negotiation.)

Overcoming Procrastination. Albert Ellis, Ph.D. William J. Knaus, Ed.D. Signet Books, 1977. (A scientific method for ending a habit that is robbing you of time, money, power, freedom, and life.)

Mentors and Proteges. Linda Phillips-Jones Arbor House, 1982. (How to establish, strengthen and get the most from a mentor/protege relationship.)

Affirmations for the Inner Child. Rokelle Lerner Health Communication, Inc., 1990. (Healing your childhood wounds and moving from a life of pain into the path of recovery.)

You, Too, Can Be Prosperous. Robert A. Russell De Vorss & Co., Publishers, 1950. (Studies in prosperity.)

The Philosophy of Moral Development. Lawrence Kohlberg Harper & Row, Publishers, 1981. (Essays on moral development.)

Psycho-Cybernetics. Maxwell Maltz, M.D.,F.I.C.S. Pocket Books, 1960. (A program for health and success.)

Unconditional Love. John Powell S.J.. Argus Communications, 1978. (The meaning and dynamics of unconditional love.)

Fully Human Fully Alive. John Powell, S.J.. Argus Communications, 1976. (A new life through a new vision.)

Psychosynthesis. Roberto Assagioli, M.D.. Franciscan Herald Press, 1975. (Integrating spiritual, mental, and emotional patterns.)

Whole - Brain Thinking. Jaquelyn Wonder & Pricilla Donovan Ballantine Books, 1984. (Working from both sides if the brain to achieve peak job performance.)

Unconditional Love and Forgiveness. Edith R. Stauffer Ph.D. Triangle Publishers,1987.

Working Without A Net. Morris R. Schechtman Pocket Books, 1994. (How to Survive & Thrive in today's high risk business world.)

Toward A Psychology Of Being. Abraham H. Maslow D. Dan Nostrand company, 1968. (An Insight Book.)

The Nibble Theory. Kaliel Jamison Paulist Press,1984. (Leadership, self-empowerment and personal growth.)

The Missing Piece. Shel Silverstein Harper & Row Publishers, 1976. (A fable on finding your missing piece.)

First Things First. Stephen R. Covey Simon & Schuster, 1994. (Relationships & results rather than time and things.)